Living in Christ

Catholic Social Teaching

Christian Life in Society

Brian Singer-Towns

saint mary's press

The Subcommittee on the Catechism, United States Conference of Catholic Bishops, has found that this catechetical high school text, copyright 2012, is in conformity with the *Catechism of the Catholic Church* and that it fulfills the requirements of Elective Course option C: "Living as a Disciple of Jesus Christ in Society" of the *Doctrinal Elements of a Curriculum Framework for the Development of Catechetical Materials for Young People of High School Age.*

Nihil Obstat: Rev. William M. Becker, STD
                       Censor Librorum
                       October 11, 2011

Imprimatur: †   Most Rev. John M. Quinn, DD
                       Bishop of Winona
                       October 11, 2011

The nihil obstat and imprimatur are official declarations that a book or pamphlet is free of doctrinal or moral error. No implication is contained therein that those who have granted the nihil obstat or imprimatur agree with the contents, opinions, or statements expressed, nor do they assume any legal responsibility associated with publication.

The publishing team included Brian Singer-Towns, development editor; Maura Thompson Hagarty, PhD, contributing editor and theological reviewer; Gloria Shahin, editorial director. Prepress and manufacturing coordinated by the production departments of Saint Mary's Press.

Cover Image: © The Crosiers / Gene Plaisted, OSC

The publisher also wishes to thank the following individuals who advised the publishing team or reviewed the work in progress:
Mary Hansel Parlin, MS, Mankato State University
Stephen M. Colecchi, DMin, St. Mary's Seminary and University, Baltimore

Printed in the United States of America

1153 (PO5941)

ISBN 978-1-59982-077-4, Print

Contents

Section 2: Creating a Just Society

Section 3: Respecting Human Life and Dignity

Section 4: The Just Distribution of Material Goods

Section 5: Living Justly

Introduction

Jesus' two Great Commandments call us to be lovers: "You shall love the Lord, your God, with all your heart, with all your soul, and with all your mind. This is the greatest and the first commandment. The second is like it: You shall love your neighbor as yourself" (Matthew 22:37–39). The Church's commitment to social justice is based on these commandments. Working for greater justice in society is a concrete expression of our love of our neighbor that flows from our love of God. Every disciple of Christ is called to be engaged in this work of faith.

Working for justice has been very important in strengthening my relationship with God. The wisdom in the Church's social teaching documents has enriched my understanding of our faith. The frustrations that come when working for justice have called me to be more patient and to rely more on God's grace. The joy of seeing people's lives improve has made me more grateful and hopeful. And working with other Catholics on justice projects has helped me to see the Holy Spirit at work in the life of the Church. I know that as you participate in the Church's work for charity and justice, your relationship with God will grow too.

I wish to express my gratitude to Dr. Stephen M. Colecchi and Mary Hansel Parlin, who reviewed the manuscript for this book, offering many helpful suggestions for improving the content. They are two gifted teachers and their commitment to the Church's social mission has inspired many people, including me.

Blessings,
Brian Singer-Towns

Foundational Principles of Social Justice

Part 1

Social Justice and God's Plan

Upon signing the Declaration of Independence, Benjamin Franklin is reported to have said, "Gentlemen, we must all hang together, or most assuredly we will all hang separately." This was a clever way of saying that if the signers of the declaration did not support one another in the endeavor to become an independent nation, the leaders of the British Empire would have them arrested and executed one by one. Franklin's statement implicitly recognized that some important changes require a communal response. This is certainly true when confronting sins that are embedded in society.

This is but one example of a simple but profound truth recognized throughout history: God created human beings to be social creatures. God is a communion of Three Divine Persons who are in eternal, loving relationship with one another. Human beings are made in his image. We cannot exist as solitary beings and still achieve God's ultimate purpose for our lives: to live in loving communion with God and with one another. And if we are to have loving communion with God and other people, our relationships must be rooted in love and justice.

This first part of section 1 builds a solid foundation for discussing and understanding social justice issues and concerns. The articles look at the social dimension of God's original plan for human beings, the social dimensions of his plan for salvation after Adam and Eve's Original Sin, and the Church's identity as loving communion and as a just community. These articles touch on topics you have previously studied, but they do so from a unique perspective: the perspective of the social nature of human beings and the responsibilities that flow from that nature.

The articles in this part address the following topics:

Article 1 God's Original Plan: A Just Community

genocide
The systematic and planned extermination of an entire ethnic, religious, political, or cultural group of people.

Here is a disturbing fact. According to the History Place Web site, during the last century there have been more than twenty documented genocides throughout the world, resulting in the deaths of more than twenty million people. A **genocide** is an attempt to destroy an entire people—an ethnic group or a religious group, for example—by killing every man, woman, and child in that group. These twenty million deaths did not occur because of a war, although war is often the excuse for, or the result of, genocide. These deaths occurred because one group of people decided that another group of people did not deserve to exist.

The excuses used to justify genocides are many. The group being killed might be labeled enemies of the aggressors, or they are being blamed for a societal problem or natural catastrophe, or perhaps something in their way of life is declared to be an immoral or evil influence in society. Whatever the excuse, the people doing the killing are overlooking a foundational religious truth: Every human person is created in the image of God. The great evil of genocide and other social injustices can happen only when people deny the most basic of truths that flow from God's purpose in creating human beings. This article reviews some of the truths that must be respected for just societies to exist.

God's Plan for Humanity

The Creation accounts in the first chapters of the Book of Genesis reveal important truths about the role justice plays in God's plan for human beings. The first truth is that God has given human beings a share of his divine life, creating us "in the divine image" (Genesis 1:27). We see further evidence for this truth in the second Creation account, when God shared his divine breath with the first man in order to bring him to life (see 2:7). Because human beings share in God's life, we are unique among all creatures; each human life has great value. Therefore justice requires us to recognize and respect the divine presence in every human being (see Matthew 25:37–40).

A second truth revealed in the Creation accounts is that human beings are religious beings. The desire for God is part of our very nature, and our true purpose is to seek for the truth and happiness that only God can provide. We were created to live in communion with God, who alone is the source of our true happiness. This is symbolized in the accounts of God's presence with Adam and Eve in the Garden of Eden (see Genesis 2:15–17, 3:8–9). In the garden God revealed himself directly to Adam and Eve, spoke to them, and gave himself to them in love without any difficulties or barriers. Their happiness flowed directly from this intimate friendship with God. We call this the state of **original holiness and justice**. Even after humanity lost the state of original holiness and justice because of Adam and Eve's first sin, God never ceased loving human beings and continued to reveal himself and give himself to us.

A third truth revealed in the Creation accounts is that God created human beings to live in loving communion with one another. The *Catechism of the Catholic Church (CCC)* expresses the need for human beings to live in community: "The human person needs to live in society. Society is not for him an extraneous addition but a requirement of his nature" (1879).

In the second account of Creation, God preceded the creation of the first woman by saying, "It is not good for the man to be alone" (Genesis 2:18). The creation of Eve from one of Adam's ribs symbolizes the intimate connection that

original holiness
The original state of human beings in their relationship with God, sharing in the divine life in full communion with him.

original justice
The state of complete harmony of our first parents with themselves, with each other, and with all of creation.

How do the accounts of Creation in the Book of Genesis reveal God's desire for us to live in loving communion with him and with other human beings?

Elio Ciol/CORBIS

common good

The good that is collectively shared by a number of people and that is beneficial for all members of a given community. Social conditions that allow for all citizens of the earth, individuals and families, to meet basic needs and achieve fulfillment promote the common good.

Fall, the

Also called the Fall from Grace, the biblical revelation about the origins of sin and evil in the world, expressed figuratively in the account of Adam and Eve in Genesis.

Original Sin

The sin by which the first humans disobeyed God and thereby lost original holiness and became subject to death. Original Sin is transmitted to every person born into the world, except Mary and Jesus.

should exist between human beings as part of God's plan. The partnership of a man and a woman is the prototype—the original model or foundation—for the loving friendship that God intends to exist between all human beings. From this follows God's plan that requires human beings to build communities of love and justice and work together for the **common good.** The primary community is the family, and all other communities are built upon and support the family. In particular the Church, the Body of Christ, is a community of love and justice with Christ as our head.

The Breakdown of God's Plan

What happens when human beings do not respect that every human person is made in God's image and likeness, when they do not trust in God for their happiness, and when they do not build communities of love and peace? The account of **the Fall** gives us insight into this question. When Adam and Eve ate the forbidden fruit, they did not respect the truths about justice revealed in the Creation accounts.

First, they doubted that they shared in God's divine life. Recall how the serpent tempted Eve to eat the fruit: "God knows well that the moment you eat of it your eyes will be opened and you will be like gods" (Genesis 3:5). We know that Eve was already like God, made in his image, but the serpent tempted her to believe that she did not really share in the divine life.

Second, Adam and Eve's sin of disobedience showed their lack of trust in God for all they needed to be happy. They abused their God-given freedom and set themselves against God, believing they could find their true happiness apart from him.

Third, in committing their sin, Adam and Eve did not live out a relationship based in love, and they did not work together for their common good. For example, Adam did not try to protect Eve from doing wrong by dissuading her from eating the fruit. And after Eve ate the fruit, she invited Adam to join in her disobedience, offering the fruit to him to eat, which he willingly did.

The effect of Adam and Eve's disobedience was that they lost their state of original holiness and justice. And they lost it not only for themselves but also for all human beings coming after them, with the exception of Mary, Jesus'

After Cain killed Abel, the Lord asked him, "Where is your brother?" and Cain replied, "Am I my brother's keeper?" How would you answer this question based on Jesus' teachings?

© Arte & Immagini srl/CORBIS

mother, and, of course, Jesus himself. **Original Sin** is the loss of our original holiness and justice—it is the wounded human nature that is transmitted to all people as a result of Adam and Eve's first sin. Because of Original Sin, our human nature is weakened in its powers. We are subject to ignorance, suffering, and death, and it is harder for us to resist the temptation to sin. We see these results in the biblical accounts that directly follow Adam and Eve's expulsion from the Garden of Eden, starting with Cain and Abel.

Chapter 4 of Genesis tells us about the relationship of Adam and Eve's sons, Cain and Abel. Cain and Abel's relationship was marked by jealousy rather than by loving communion. Overcome by feelings of resentment and anger toward his brother, Cain was unable to resist the temptation to kill Abel and thus committed the first murder, which was also an act of injustice. Weakened by Original Sin, Cain was unwilling to recognize that both he and Abel shared in God's life and that he must protect his brother's life, not take it.

social justice
The defense of human dignity by ensuring that essential human needs are met and that essential human rights are protected for all people.

From there, things only got worse. Genesis goes on to describe how generations went by and human beings and their sins multiplied—until we get to Noah (see Genesis, chapters 6–9). From the story of Noah, we learn that almost all of humanity, weakened by Original Sin, was engulfed in sin and injustice. Genesis tells us: "In the eyes of God the earth was corrupt and full of lawlessness. . . . God saw how corrupt the earth had become, since all mortals led depraved lives on earth" (6:11–12). God had no choice except to begin again, destroying all life except for Noah, his family, and the animals they brought with them on the ark.

From these accounts we learn an important religious truth: the loss of our original holiness and justice can easily lead to evil and corrupt societies. But there is good news too, as we learn from Noah's story; God's salvation is near to those who remember him and who remain faithful to his original plan in creating humankind. ✝

A Summary of the Social Justice Principles in the Creation Accounts

The truths revealed in the first chapters of Genesis lead to these important principles for **social justice:**

- Because human beings are made in the image and likeness of God, each human life has great worth and must be protected. Therefore societies must not place greater value on prestige, power, or material goods than on human life.

- Because our true happiness comes from God and from God alone, human beings cannot find the happiness they long for by pursuing things that do not lead us to God. Societies must not promote the belief that true happiness can be found in things such as fame, success, or the accumulation of material goods but must instead promote values that emphasize the inherent worth of each individual.

- Because God intends that human beings form communities of love and justice that work together for the common good, we must have the same concern for other people's welfare that we do for our own. Therefore societies must be committed to the common good; power and wealth must not be concentrated in the hands of a privileged few.

These principles are foundational to the Church's mission to be an instrument of God's justice in the world.

Article 2 The Social Dimension of God's Plan of Salvation

> The heavens proclaim God's justice;
> all peoples see his glory.
>
> (Psalm 97:6)

How do we know that our God demands justice? Human beings can know God with certainty by his works and by our own use of human reason. But Original Sin has clouded our reason and our ability to know God through the natural world, so he has also gradually revealed himself and his saving plan through mighty works and words. This **Divine Revelation** is communicated through Sacred Scripture and Sacred Tradition. Together **Scripture** and **Tradition** "make up a single sacred deposit of the Word of God" (*Dei Verbum*, 10; in *CCC*, 97), through which the Church comes to know the one, true God and understand his will.

Scripture and Tradition reveal how God has been at work throughout human history to save humanity from sin and death and restore our original holiness and justice. The Church calls this pattern of saving events **salvation history.** The **covenants** that God makes with humanity are a crucial part of salvation history, and they help us to understand how God's saving plan unfolds. This article reviews those covenants, pointing out their social dimensions. God is just and calls us to love others and to build communities that practice justice.

The Covenants with Noah and Abraham

The covenants of the Old Testament, even though they were often made between God and a particular person, reveal God's respect for all life and his concern for justice. Consider the first explicit covenant in the Old Testament, the Covenant God made with Noah (see Genesis 9:1–17). This was the heart of that Covenant: "I will establish my covenant with you, that never again shall all bodily creatures be destroyed by the waters of a flood; there shall not be another flood to devastate the earth. . . . This is the sign that I am giving for all ages to come, of the covenant between me and you and every living creature with you: I set my bow in the clouds to serve as a sign of the covenant between me and

Divine Revelation

God's self-communication through which he makes known the mystery of his divine plan. Divine Revelation is a gift accomplished by the Father, Son, and Holy Spirit through the words and deeds of salvation history. It is most fully realized in the Passion, death, Resurrection, and Ascension of Jesus Christ.

Scripture(s)

Generally, the term for any sacred writing. For Christians, the Old and New Testaments that make up the Bible and are recognized as the Word of God.

Tradition

This word (from the Latin meaning "to hand on") refers to the process of passing on the Gospel message. Tradition, which began with the oral communication of the Gospel by the Apostles, was written down in the Scriptures, is handed down and lived out in the life of the Church, and is interpreted by the bishops of the Church in union with the Pope under the guidance of the Holy Spirit.

salvation history
The pattern of specific salvific events in human history in which God clearly reveals his presence and saving actions. Salvation was accomplished once and for all through Jesus Christ, a truth foreshadowed and revealed throughout the Old Testament.

covenant
A solemn agreement between human beings or between God and a human being in which mutual commitments are made.

the earth" (9:11–13). This Covenant clearly shows God's love and respect for all life, because God extended its saving promise not just to Noah but to all living beings for as long as the world lasts.

The Covenant with Noah also placed additional social demands on Noah and all human beings who have come after him:

> For your own lifeblood, too, I will demand an accounting:
> from every animal I will demand it, and from man in regard to
> his fellow man I will demand an accounting for human life.
>   If anyone sheds the blood of man,
>   by man shall his blood be shed;
>   For in the image of God
>   has man been made.
>
> (9:5–6)

In these verses we see that God calls all human beings to respect the lives of other people. If you harm another person (shed his or her blood), God will hold you accountable for that death or injury. The Covenant with Noah calls us to respect and care for all human life.

The next Old Testament covenant is the Covenant God made with Abraham. In this Covenant God began the formation of his Chosen People. Variations of this Covenant are found in Genesis 12:1–3, 15:1–22, and 17:1–22. These passages describe the three promises that God made to

Abraham: (1) the promise of numerous descendents who would become a great nation, (2) the promise of a land for Abraham and his descendents to call their own, and (3) the promise that "all the communities of the earth / shall find blessing" in Abraham (12:3). The third promise is understood in two ways, and both understandings have important social dimensions. First, it is understood as a promise that Abraham and his descendents would be a blessing to other nations and groups of people through their faith in the one, true God. Through the example they set for others in living out their faith, they have also shown other people how to live in just and peaceful societies.

© Vanni/Art Resource, NY

This early Christian image (circa AD 330) depicts both the Nativity and the sacrifice of Isaac. Why do you think these two biblical accounts were selected to appear side by side in this image?

Second, Christians understand it as a promise that has been fulfilled through Jesus Christ forever. Christ is a direct descendent of Abraham (see Matthew 1:1). God has fully revealed himself in and through him. Through Christ's Passion, death, Resurrection, and Ascension, all people, of every race and nation, are "blessed." Through faith in Christ, any person can regain his or her original holiness and justice and live in loving communion with others. Christ's disciples will form the Church and she, like the Israelites, will be an example for all in building communities of justice and peace.

The Sinai Covenant

The next Old Testament covenant is the Covenant God made with the Israelites at Mount Sinai. The Sinai Covenant, also called the Mosaic Covenant, was made during the Exodus from Egypt. The Exodus itself was an event with important implications for social justice. After settling in Egypt as welcome immigrants, the Israelites had become enslaved by

Old Law

Divine Law revealed in the Old Testament, summarized in the Ten Commandments. Also called the Law of Moses. It is succeeded by the New Law of the Gospels.

the Egyptian empire. When the Israelites cried out to God, he had compassion for them because of their unjust suffering. God sent Moses as his messenger to confront Pharaoh and delivered the Israelites from their enslavement with mighty deeds (see Exodus, chapters 1–15). From the Exodus accounts, we learn that God is on the side of those who have been unjustly treated—often called the oppressed—and that nations or groups that treat others unjustly lose his favor.

As part of the Sinai Covenant, God gave the Israelites laws to live by. According to the biblical account, Moses

Pray It!

Prayers for Justice in the Psalms

Many of the Psalms proclaim God's desire for justice. Here are two examples. Perhaps you can make these Psalms part of your own prayer.

The LORD rules forever,
    has set up a throne for judgment.
It is God who governs the world with justice,
    who judges the peoples with fairness.
The LORD is a stronghold for the oppressed,
    a stronghold in times of trouble.
                (Psalm 9:8–10)

Happy those whose help is Jacob's God,
    whose hope is in the LORD, their God,
The maker of heaven and earth,
    the seas and all that is in them,
Who keeps faith forever,
    secures justice for the oppressed,
    gives food to the hungry.
The LORD sets prisoners free;
    the LORD gives sight to the blind.
The LORD raises up those who are bowed down;
    the LORD loves the righteous.
The LORD protects the stranger,
    sustains the orphan and the widow,
    but thwarts the way of the wicked.
The LORD shall reign forever,
    your God, Zion, through all generations!
Hallelujah!
                (Psalm 146:5–10)

delivered the laws to the Israelites at Mount Sinai (see Exodus, chapters 19–40), delivered another version of laws sometime later from the meeting tent (see the Book of Leviticus), and summarized the laws again before his death (see the Book of Deuteronomy). These laws are summarized by the Ten Commandments (see Exodus, chapter 20) and are often called the **Old Law** to distinguish them from the **New Law** of Christ. Many Scripture scholars believe that these collections of laws developed over many years, even centuries, before they were recorded as we have them in the Bible.

God gave his Law to the Israelites to teach them how to live as holy people, his Chosen People. The Old Law contains laws about worship of God, ritual purity, sexual morality, and just behavior in society. The laws governing just behavior are of particular interest to our study of social justice and are discussed in article 5, "Social Teaching in the Old Testament." Here is a brief summary of some those laws:

- One must not cause another person physical harm. If someone does injure or kill another human being, even accidentally or through negligence, a just recompense must be made for the harm done.

- One must act fairly in financial affairs and must not profit from someone else's misfortune.

- The natural resources people need to survive must be fairly distributed. When the ownership of natural resources becomes unbalanced, they must periodically be redistributed.

- One must treat foreigners, widows, orphans, and other people in poverty with compassion and generosity.

The Old Law was a step in God's plan, the first stage of revealed law. It was meant to teach the Israelites how to live holy and just lives. But it was insufficient on its own to bring

New Law
Divine Law revealed in the New Testament through the life and teaching of Jesus Christ and through the witness and teaching of the Apostles. The New Law perfects the Old Law and brings it to fulfillment. Also called the Law of Love.

Of the many events from Moses' life portrayed in this image, why are the Commandments the central focus?

© Malcah Zeldis / Art Resource, NY

salvation to humanity. Saint Paul called the Old Law a disciplinarian; it prepared us for the fullness of salvation that is found through faith in Jesus Christ:

> Before faith came, we were held in custody under law, confined for the faith that was to be revealed. Consequently, the law was our disciplinarian for Christ, that we might be justified by faith. But now that faith has come, we are no longer under a disciplinarian. For through faith you are all children of God in Christ Jesus. (Galatians 3:23–26) ✝

Article 3 The Social Dimension of the Paschal Mystery

A priest who was well known both as a pastor and as an advocate for social justice was sometimes asked about his commitment to social justice. "Your stances on social justice issues sometimes make people uncomfortable, even angry" said one questioner. "Shouldn't you just be concerned about people's spiritual lives? Why do you need to mix politics with religion?"

The priest had a reply ready. He stated:

> Christ came to comfort the afflicted and to afflict the comfortable. He challenged the people of his time to be compassion givers, justice builders, and peace makers, which made him unpopular with some people. His obedience to his Father's will made it possible for all people to know the peace and joy of the Kingdom of God. And even though we will know the perfection of the Kingdom only when we get to Heaven, God doesn't ask us to wait until we get to Heaven to have a taste of his Kingdom. The Holy Spirit empowers us to participate in building the Kingdom of God and to be its ambassadors. Our Baptism calls us to cooperate with God's grace as compassion givers, justice builders, and peace makers. It is impossible for true faith to be just a private faith; true faith always has a social dimension.

Salvation and Social Justice

Some Christians insist that faith in Christ does not have a social dimension. They believe that Christ's Passion, death, Resurrection, and Ascension are for only our individual salvation. These Christians believe that faith is a personal matter and that the Church should not get involved with social issues. For them, Christian morality is concerned solely with personal moral issues, and social justice has no place in Church teaching. Though these Christians may be well intentioned, they have failed to understand a central truth of Christian faith: God's plan of salvation is both personal and communal.

Let's quickly review the essential elements of the culmination, or complete fulfillment, of God's plan for our salvation. Out of his great love for us, when the time was right, God the Father took the initiative to send his only Son to save us from sin and death and restore our holiness and justice. The Son of God, the Eternal Word who is one with the Father, assumed a human nature without losing his divine nature and was born of the Virgin Mary. The mystery of the Incarnation is the union of the human and divine natures in one Divine Person, Jesus Christ. As a teacher and a healer, Christ revealed the Kingdom of God. All of his life teaches us about God's saving plan: his poverty, his humility, his prayer, who he lived with, who he called to be his disciples, his teaching and preaching, his healings, his exorcisms, his acceptance of the cross . . . everything. In the moral realm, he gave us a New Law (summarized in the Sermon on the Mount; see Matthew, chapters 5–7) to teach humanity how to live as citizens of the Kingdom, completing the instruction that began with the Old Law.

The New Testament reveals that God's plan is fulfilled through the life and work of Jesus Christ, especially through his Passion, death, Resurrection, and Ascension. We call this the **Paschal Mystery.** As true God and true man, Jesus Christ is the one and only perfect mediator between God and humanity. He freely offered himself for our salvation in obedience to his Father's will. His suffering and his cruel death—real in every respect—bought forgiveness for the sins of all humanity. His Resurrection—a historical reality confirmed by his disciples who encountered the Risen Christ—affirms that everything Jesus taught and promised is true, particularly his promise that those who believe in him will conquer death and share in his resurrected life. At his Ascension, Jesus, still retaining his humanity, entered Heaven and prepared the way for the coming of the Holy Spirit. The Holy

Paschal Mystery
The work of salvation accomplished by Jesus Christ mainly through his Passion, death, Resurrection, and Ascension.

Spirit is poured out by Christ on the members of the Church to call us to conversion, to empower us for service, and to help us to grow in holiness. At the end of time, Christ will come again to judge the living and the dead; he will reward the just who accepted his grace and punish the unjust who refused to cooperate with his grace.

The Paschal Mystery is the fulfillment of the New Covenant that God makes with all people. The New Covenant fulfills all the promises of the Old Covenant. In the New Covenant, God extends the forgiveness of sin and the promise of eternal life to people of every race and nation. For people to enter into the New Covenant, they must place their faith in Jesus Christ, be baptized, and follow Christ's New Law of Love.

The New Law of Love is where the social dimension of the Gospel enters, for the New Law of Christ requires us to be compassionate toward others and to live justly. It requires that we respect the life and dignity of every person, share our material goods to help other people in need, and build just societies that protect the essential rights of all people. Specific teachings of the New Law that pertain to these responsibilities are covered in article 7, "Social Teaching in the New Testament." For now, reflect on these two New Testament quotations about living justly:

© Brian Singer-Towns/Saint Mary's Press

How does Jesus call us to act with love and justice through his teachings and the Paschal Mystery?

Not everyone who says to me, "Lord, Lord," will enter the kingdom of heaven, but only the one who does the will of my Father in heaven. (Matthew 7:21)

What good is it, my brothers, if someone says he has faith but does not have works? Can that faith save him? If a brother or sister has nothing to wear and has no food for the day, and one of you says to them, "Go in peace, keep warm, and eat well," but you do not give them the necessities of the body, what good is it? So also faith of itself, if it does not have works, is dead. (James 2:14–17)

Jesus' Teachings on Social Justice

Throughout his active ministry, through his words and actions, Jesus' teachings on social justice challenged many of the contemporary norms regarding the rich and the poor, the powerful and the powerless, the "haves and have-nots." In Jesus' time, it was believed that wealth was a sign of special favor from God, and that sickness and suffering were retribution from God for sin. Jesus instead taught that the wealthy must not see themselves as superior or favored by God, but must instead share their material goods with the poor (see Luke 16:19–25) and that those in power have a responsibility to use their power in service to others (see Matthew 20:25–27). In the Parable of the Rich Man and Lazarus (Luke 16:19–25), Jesus tells of a rich man who dressed in fine clothes and dined on sumptuous meals every day while a beggar named Lazarus lay at his door hungry and sick. When the two die, Lazarus rejoices with the angels while the rich man is tormented with suffering, because he refused to share his material comforts during his life on earth. On another occasion, when there was disagreement among the Apostles about who was the greatest among them, Jesus reminded them that unlike those in the world who lord their power over others, they are called to greatness by serving others. He tells them, "Whoever wishes to be first among you shall be your slave" (Matthew 20:25). In other words, whoever humbly serves others will be truly great in God's Kingdom.

There are also countless examples in the Gospels of Jesus caring for those who are poor or overlooked in society, and of his call to us to do the same. Jesus cures the blind and the lame (see, for example, Matthew 15:30–32), he shows mercy to the sinner (see, for example, Luke 19:1–10), and he repeatedly calls us to treat others with the same love and mercy he shows us (see, for example, John 13:34).

Individual Salvation but a Communal Process

The Paschal Mystery teaches us that our salvation has both individual and communal dimensions. The individual dimension flows from the truth that each person's salvation is based on his or her personal decisions and actions. Each of us has to decide to cooperate with God's grace and put our faith in Christ and commit to being a member of the Body of Christ. Each of us must make decisions to participate in the Sacraments, make good moral choices, serve others, and live a just life. No one can decide this for us, and no one can completely take this choice away from us (although someone could make it more difficult).

The communal dimension of salvation flows from the truth that the process of salvation is based in community. When people respond to God's call and become members of the Church, they commit to following Christ and become part of a communion with one another, a communion that is rooted in union with God. The members of the Church rely on one another's support in living holy lives. They participate in the Sacraments as a community, and through the Sacraments they are united as one family. Guided by the Holy Spirit, the members of the Church are a loving community that models for the world what it is like to live as a just and peaceful society. The decision to follow Christ is an individual one, but the result of that personal decision is that we belong to and participate in a community, the Body of Christ.

As members of the Church, we continue Christ's saving mission, reaching out to the entire human community. Our commitment to social justice flows directly from this mission. In 2005 Pope Benedict XVI said:

> As the years went by and the Church spread further afield, the exercise of charity became established as one of her essential activities, along with the administration of the sacraments and the proclamation of the word: love for widows and orphans, prisoners, and the sick and needy of every kind, is as essential to her as the ministry of the sacraments and preaching of the Gospel. The Church cannot neglect the service of charity any more than she can neglect the Sacraments and the Word. (*God Is Love [Deus Caritas Est]*, 22)

Catholic Wisdom

Salvation Has Always Been Considered a Social Reality

Pope Benedict XVI offers the following short reflection on the communal nature of salvation.

> The *Letter to the Hebrews* speaks of a "city" (cf. 11:10, 16; 12:22; 13:14) and therefore of communal salvation. Consistently with this view, sin is understood by the [Church] Fathers as the destruction of the unity of the human race, as fragmentation and division. . . . Hence "redemption" appears as the reestablishment of unity, in which we come together once more in a union that begins to take shape in the world community of believers. (*On Christian Hope*, 14)

© istock/Christopher Futcher

"For where two or three are gathered together in my name, there am I in the midst of them" (Matthew 18:20).

Trinity

From the Latin *trinus*, meaning "threefold," referring to the central mystery of the Christian faith that God exists as a communion of three distinct and interrelated Divine Persons: Father, Son, and Holy Spirit. The doctrine of the Trinity is a mystery that is inaccessible to human reason alone and is known through Divine Revelation only.

Thus, a commitment to social justice, when it is properly understood, is an essential part of Christian life. It was part of God's original plan for humanity and is taught in both his Old Law and his New Law. God expects us to care for the good of others just as much as we care for our own good. However challenging or uncomfortable it might make us, God even expects us to sacrifice our comfort, our wealth, and perhaps even our lives to protect other people's lives and rights and to ensure that their essential human needs are met. ✝

Article 4   The Church: Communion and a Just Community

People who participate in church activities often experience close relationships with the groups they are involved in. These relationships can develop during retreats, conferences, work camps, Mass, and so on. We are able to develop these relationships through God's grace. Our communion with one another should resemble the communion of the Holy **Trinity.** The Three Divine Persons of the Trinity, the Father, Son, and Holy Spirit, are in perfect, loving relationship with one another. Through God's grace the Church is the sacrament of the Holy Trinity's communion with humanity; that is, the Church is both a sign of true communion and the cause of our communion. Through God's grace the Church is a true communion of persons, a community of love, truth, and justice.

Church

The term *Church* has three inseparable meanings: (1) the entire People of God throughout the world; (2) the diocese, which is also known as the local Church; and (3) the assembly of believers gathered for the celebration of the liturgy, especially the Eucharist. In the Nicene Creed, the Church is recognized as One, Holy, Catholic, and Apostolic—traits that together are referred to as "marks of the Church."

The Sacrament of Salvation

Christ founded the **Church** as both the means and the goal of his saving mission. The Church is the *means* God uses for fulfilling his plan of salvation because the members of the Church witness to the saving power of the Paschal Mystery. When Christians practice their love for one another and their compassion for those who are suffering and in need, they are witnessing to Christ's love alive in their lives. This witness helps others to understand what the love of God truly is and encourages them to put their faith in Christ. Loving and compassionate witness includes speaking out for justice and advocating for moral issues as a disciple of Jesus Christ.

But the Church, when she is brought to perfection by grace of God, is also the *goal* of God's plan. When Christians practice all the things that Jesus requires in the New Law—sacrificial love, forgiveness, prayer, a commitment to live justly, and so on—their actions are signs that the seed of the Kingdom of God on earth has been planted in the Church. When God brings this seed to its full fruition, there will be no injustice: no hunger, no inequality, no prejudice, no poverty, and no disrespect for God's gift of life. At the end of time, when the Kingdom of God is fully realized, all the People of God will be gathered together in communion with God and with one another in the perfected Church.

© The Gallery Collection/Corbis

Another way of saying this is that "the Church in this world is the sacrament of salvation, the sign and the instrument of the communion of God and men" (*CCC*, 780). A sacrament is both a sign and a cause of God's **grace**. As the sacrament of salvation, the Church is both a sign of God's saving power and the cause that makes God's saving power real in the world.

Some people disagree with the idea that the Church helps to bring about the growth of the Kingdom of God here on earth. They point out times in the Church's history when members of the Church persecuted others, sometimes committing

Ecumenism and Social Justice

Despite differences in doctrinal beliefs, Catholics and other Christians have found common ground in working and advocating for justice and peace. By doing so we grow in our understanding and respect for our brothers and sisters in Christ. Reflect on this passage from the Second Vatican Council's *Decree on Ecumenism* (*Unitatis Redintegratio*), which urges Catholics to work together with other Christians on social issues:

> In these days when cooperation in social matters is so widespread . . . cooperation among Christians vividly expresses the relationship which in fact already unites them, and it sets in clearer relief the features of Christ the Servant. This cooperation, which has already begun in many countries, should be developed more and more, particularly in regions where a social and technical evolution is taking place be it in a just evaluation of the dignity of the human person, the establishment of the blessings of peace, the application of Gospel principles to social life, the advancement of the arts and sciences in a truly Christian spirit, or also in the use of various remedies to relieve the afflictions of our times such as famine and natural disasters, illiteracy and poverty, housing shortage and the unequal distribution of wealth. All believers in Christ can, through this cooperation, be led to acquire a better knowledge and appreciation of one another, and so pave the way to Christian unity. (12)

horrible atrocities in the name of the Church. They point to leaders in the Church who have committed terrible sins. They point to ordinary people in their parishes who sometimes act unjustly or unkindly. All of these things have been true and are a scandal to the mission of the Church. Sin is a reality among the members of the Church; thus the Church on earth is an imperfect taste of the perfect communion that awaits us in the Kingdom of God. Still, through the power of the Holy Spirit, the Church is the seed and the beginning of the Kingdom on earth and gives us a glimpse of the Kingdom of God, which will come in fullness at the end of time.

Just as Jesus is one Divine Person with two natures, human and divine, so too the Church is one reality formed of two dimensions: the human and the divine. Knowing that the Church has a visible reality and a spiritual reality is

grace

The free and undeserved gift of God's loving and active presence in the universe and in our lives, empowering us to respond to his call and to live as his adopted sons and daughters. Grace restores our loving communion with the Holy Trinity, lost through sin.

essential in understanding how the Church can be a sacrament of the Kingdom of God despite the sin of her members. Any person—whether a believer in the Church or not—can see the visible signs of a hierarchical society: church buildings; the Pope, bishops, priests, and deacons; people attending Mass; groups doing service projects; families praying together; and so on. But only a person with faith can accept the invisible but very real spiritual dimension of the Church. In the spiritual dimension, the Holy Trinity is at work to save and make holy the human race—and God will not fail in this saving work.

Describing the Church's Communion

Many of the ways we describe the Church express some aspect of the communion of the members of the Church with one another and with God. The word *Church* means "convocation." A convocation is a group of people who have been called together for a special purpose. The Church is called together by the Holy Spirit to be the People of God. As the People of God, we are fed by the Body of Christ, the Eucharist, so that we might become the living Body of Christ. The Body of Christ as a description of the Church comes from the New Testament epistles. In First Corinthians, chapter 12, Saint Paul uses the analogy of the human body to explain that the members of the Church must work together for the common good just as the different parts of the human body all work together. The Letter to the Ephesians states that Christ is the head of this Body: "Rather, living the truth in love, we should grow in every way into him who is the head, Christ" (4:15). Thus the Church lives for and with Christ, and he lives with and in the Church. Describing the Church as the Body of Christ helps us to understand that she has diversity among her members and their functions and that these diverse members work together, supporting one another in building a community of love and justice, and continuing the mission of Jesus Christ.

The Church is also sometimes called the Mystical Body of Christ. Adding the word *mystical* to the description emphasizes that the Church has an unseen, spiritual dimension. The Church also includes all the saints who have died before us and are now with God in Heaven. The members of the Church alive at the present time are not just

© Brian Singer-Towns/Saint Mary's Press

This painting depicts the Mystical Body of Christ, the saints both in Heaven and on earth. What does the doctrine of the Mystical Body of Christ imply about how we should treat one another?

in communion with one another and with Jesus Christ, our head; we are in communion with all the holy members of the Church who have died before us.

Another popular name for the Church is the Family of God. This is another biblical image that comes from the New Testament writings. It is based on the truth that God is our heavenly Father and that his only Son, Jesus Christ, is our brother. This means that the members of the Church must

Pray It!

Pope Benedict Prays for Peace and Justice

Pope Benedict XVI ended an Advent talk with this beautiful prayer for peace and justice. Let it be a model for your own personal prayer.

Dear friends, in this preparation for Christmas, now at hand, the Church's prayer for the fulfillment of the hopes of peace, salvation and justice which the world today urgently needs becomes more intense. Let us ask God to grant that violence be overcome by the power of love, that opposition give way to reconciliation and that the desire to oppress be transformed into the desire for forgiveness, justice, and peace. . . . May peace be in our hearts so that they are open to the action of God's grace. . . . May all members of the family community, especially children, the elderly, the weakest, feel the warmth of this feast and may it extend subsequently to all the days in the year. Amen! ("General Audience," December 19, 2007) treat one another as beloved brothers and sisters. Jesus set the standard for this: "For whoever does the will of my heavenly Father is my brother, and sister, and mother" (Matthew 12:50).

Summary

Because the Church is a true communion, building just relationships and working for social justice are essential elements of her identity. As a sign of the Kingdom of God on earth, the Church must be a just community where the common good is a lived reality. In this way the Church is a teacher for the rest of society, showing others what it is like to live together in compassion, justice, and peace. She continues Christ's mission by being a social conscience for the world. ✝

Part Review

1. What are three truths about the nature of justice that are taught through the Creation accounts in Scripture?

2. How do the accounts of Cain and Abel and of Noah and the Flood demonstrate the impact of Original Sin on society?

3. Describe the social dimension of God's Covenant with Abraham.

4. What important truth about social justice is taught through the Exodus event?

5. Define the Paschal Mystery.

6. What is the social dimension associated with our salvation?

7. The Church is both the means and the goal of Christ's saving mission. What are the social justice implications of this truth?

8. Describe the Church in two ways that emphasize her social nature.

Part 2

The Social Teaching of the Church

Throughout her history the Church has worked tirelessly to protect human life, defend the common good, and promote justice in society. Consider that since the late 1800s, popes have written numerous encyclicals addressing social justice concerns; bishops have advocated with governments about life and justice issues; and priests, religious, and laypeople have worked together to defend the right to life, racial equality, workers' rights, peace, and many other important social concerns. The Catholic Church, through her various organizations and ministries, has provided more schools, hospitals, and programs to fight hunger and poverty than any other non-governmental institution. Catholics can be proud of their history in promoting social justice and working for the common good.

The Church's action for justice flows from Church teaching on social justice themes. Under the guidance of the Holy Spirit, the Magisterium—the bishops of the world in union with the Pope—apply God's truth to the social concerns of the day. Changing political and economic systems call for further prayer and study leading to a new application of God's truth to address these new situations. This is especially true in the last two centuries, as rapid technological progress has brought about major changes in health and medicine, political systems, economics, and warfare.

The articles in this part address the following topics:

- Article 5: Social Teaching in the Old Testament (page 32)
- Article 6: The Justice Message of the Prophets (page 36)
- Article 7: Social Teaching in the New Testament (page 38)
- Article 8: The Social Doctrine of the Church: Papal Social Teaching (page 44)
- Article 9: The Social Doctrine of the Church: The United States Conference of Catholic Bishops (page 51)
- Article 10: Defining *Justice* (page 55)

Article 5 Social Teaching in the Old Testament

The term *social justice* has come into frequent use only in the last century, but the concept of social justice is ancient. The Old Law of the Old Testament had many laws dealing with moral questions that today we would classify as social justice issues. This article gives a brief overview of the social justice themes found in these laws.

Teachings in the Old Law

The specific laws that compose the Old Law are collected mainly in the Books of Exodus, Leviticus, and Deuteronomy. As mentioned in article 2, "The Social Dimension of God's Plan of Salvation," these books contain laws about proper worship of God, laws about diet, laws about purity and impurity, laws about sexual morality, and laws governing just behavior in society. Through these various laws, God was teaching the Israelites how to be a holy people—that is, how to live in true, loving communion with him and with one another.

Though all the laws in the Old Law have a communal dimension, the laws governing just behavior in society most clearly reflect the principles that later develop into the social teaching of Christ and the Church. By identifying the major themes that emerge from these laws, we see the foundational social justice principles that Jesus elaborated on in the New Law. This article organizes the laws governing just behavior in society into five themes: respect for human life, respect for private property, honesty in business, the just distribution of wealth, and special concern for the vulnerable.

Respect for Human Life
(Exodus 21:12–32, Numbers 35:12–30)

A section of the laws in the Books of Exodus and Numbers gives the penalties for causing bodily harm or killing another person. The basic principle in these laws is that the penalty must be equal to the crime. So if someone deliberately murders another person, the murderer is sentenced to death (unless the person who is killed is a slave). Or if someone intentionally injures another person, the attacker is punished with the same injury. This is where the well-known phrase "an eye for an eye, a tooth for a tooth" comes from (see Exodus 21:23–25).

The uniqueness of these laws is that the punishments prescribed were less severe than the typical punishments at the time these laws were written. For example, if you lived during this time and someone killed a member of your family, you would most likely retaliate by attacking and killing several members of the murderer's family—or even the whole family. Or if someone blinded your brother in a fight, you would avenge the injury by killing his attacker. By making the punishment equal to the crime, the Old Law limited vengeful practices and taught a greater respect for human life.

Social Justice in the Proverbs

The Book of Proverbs has many short sayings that illustrate the Old Testament's perspective on social justice. Here is a sampling:

> False scales are an abomination to the Lord,
>> but a full weight is his delight. (11:1)

> He who trusts his riches will fall,
>> but like green leaves the just flourish. (11:28)

> Better a poor man who walks in his integrity
>> than he who is crooked in his ways and rich. (19:1)

> He who has compassion on the poor lends to the Lord,
>> and he will repay him for his good deed. (19:17)

> Injure not the poor because they are poor,
>> nor crush the needy at the gate;
> For the Lord will defend their cause,
>> and will plunder the lives of those who plunder them.
>>> (22:22–23)

> If your enemy be hungry, give him food to eat,
>> if he be thirsty, give him to drink. (25:21)

> Evil men understand nothing of justice,
>> but those who seek the Lord understand all. (28:5)

Respect for Private Property (Exodus 21:33—22:14, 23:4–5; Deuteronomy 22:1–4, 24:6)

A number of laws in the Old Law protect private property. They give penalties for stealing or causing damage to someone else's property, particularly harm to livestock, fields, orchards, and vineyards. Livestock, fields, orchards, and vineyards were the possessions necessary for a family to feed and clothe itself; by protecting these things, the laws protected a family's ability to provide for itself. Thus the Old Law taught the Israelites that the right to private property is a basic human right necessary for a person's or family's survival. But we should also note that the right to private property is not an absolute right in the Old Law. This point is explicitly made in Deuteronomy 24:6: "No one shall take a hand mill or even its upper stone as a pledge for debt, for he would be taking the debtor's sustenance as a pledge" (a hand mill is used to grind flour for bread).

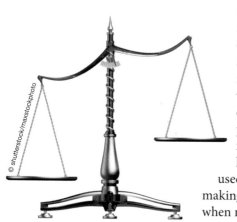

© shutterstock/maxstockphoto

Honesty in Business (Exodus 22:24–26, 23:6–8; Leviticus 19:35–36, 25:36–37; Deuteronomy 24:10–15, 25:13–16)

Several laws in the Old Law call for honesty in business practices. These laws cover a variety of topics. For example, scales were often used in business transactions because people were paid in grains or precious metal for goods and services. So there are laws commanding that honest weights be used in scales. There are also laws covering the making of loans. They forbid charging interest when making a loan to another Israelite. And if an Israelite took another Israelite's cloak as collateral for a loan, the cloak had to be returned by nightfall so the borrower would not freeze at night. There are also laws against taking bribes.

Through these laws the Old Law taught a basic social justice principle that Christ perfected in the New Law: the common good takes precedence over an individual person's right to accumulate wealth. People come before money; we must not practice dishonesty or take advantage of another person's need to make ourselves richer.

Just Distribution of Wealth
(Leviticus, chapter 25; Deuteronomy 15:1–11)

We now come to the section of the Old Law that contains the laws governing the forgiveness of debts and the redistribution of land. Deuteronomy, chapter 15, commands that in every seventh (or sabbatical) year, any financial debt that one Israelite owes another is either completely or partially forgiven (it is unclear exactly what the law required). Leviticus, chapter 25, contains an even more challenging law. Every fiftieth (or jubilee) year, all the land of Israel is to be returned to the families that originally owned it. The law required landowners to sell any land purchased in the last fifty years back to the family that originally owned it. In this way the land in Israel would be fairly distributed among the Israelites once again.

Though scholars and historians are uncertain how— or even if—these laws were observed, what the laws teach is clear: every Israelite should have access to the material goods needed to live a dignified life. The laws extend special consideration to poor Israelites to help them keep or obtain the material possessions they need to earn their own living. It is God's will that the people who have more wealth than they need share with those who are struggling to survive. The basis for these laws is the religious truth that God is the ultimate "owner" of the goods of the earth and that human beings should never consider themselves the permanent owners of the earth's resources: "The land shall not be sold in perpetuity; for the land is mine [God's], and you are but aliens who have become my tenants" (Leviticus 25:23).

UCHETA DAS/Reuters/Corbis

The Missionaries of Charity, a religious order founded by Saint Mother Teresa, devote their lives to the care of the poor and vulnerable.

prophet

A person God chooses to speak his message of salvation. In the Bible, primarily a communicator of a divine message of repentance to the Chosen People, not necessarily a person who predicted the future.

The prophet Jeremiah called the people of Israel to repent and be faithful to their Covenant with God. What message would a prophet of God have for us today?

Special Concern for the Vulnerable (Exodus 22:20–26, Leviticus 25:35–41, Deuteronomy 24:17–22)

The fifth theme is implied in the other themes but is also stated explicitly in laws found in Exodus, Leviticus, and Deuteronomy. These laws command the Israelites not to take advantage of the most vulnerable members of their society and, even more, to make special provisions for their welfare. Here is the version of the law from Deuteronomy:

> You shall not violate the rights of the alien or of the orphan, nor take the clothing of a widow as a pledge. For, remember, you were once slaves in Egypt, and the LORD, your God, ransomed you from there; that is why I command you to observe this rule. (24:17–18)

In ancient Israelite and other Middle Eastern cultures, a person's survival depended on his or her membership in a tribe or extended family. Shepherding and farming requires a group of people working together at the many tasks required to produce food, clothing, and shelter and to protect themselves from thieves and marauders. Aliens (travelers or immigrants), orphans, and widows were therefore at risk because they had no family to provide for them and protect them. Thus God commanded the Israelites to be especially attentive to their rights and to leave food for them in the fields, orchards, and vineyards.

Through these laws the Old Law taught the Israelites that it is sinful for a society to take advantage of poor and vulnerable people and sinful not to provide for their basic needs. This theme is continued in the New Law and becomes one of the distinguishing characteristics of the early Church. ✟

© Adam Woolfitt/CORBIS

Article 6 The Justice Message of the Prophets

The **prophets** of the Old Testament were the guardians of the Old Law. When the Israelites failed to keep the Commandments of the Sinai Covenant, the prophets spoke for God, reminding kings and peasants what the Law required them to do. The prophets called the Israelites to put their total trust in God, to turn away from false gods and goddesses, to be authentic in their worship, to repent of their sins and turn back to God, and to practice justice in their relationships with one another. This chart lists key passages of the social justice teachings of the prophets. ✝

Key Passages Highlighting the Social Justice Message of the Prophets	
Passage	**Summary of Prophet's Message**
Isaiah 1:11–16, 21–23; 2:13–15	God condemns the kingdoms of Israel and Judah: Their religious observances are empty of meaning because they have failed to act justly and they mistreat people who are poor and vulnerable.
Isaiah 58:5–11	God declares the fasting he desires is the freedom of oppressed people and the care of those in need.
Jeremiah 22:1–17	God warns the kings of Judah that he will bring their kingdom to ruin if they do not act justly, care for the vulnerable, respect human life, and give workers their fair wages.
Hosea 12:8–9	God condemns those who use dishonest scales in order to increase their wealth.
Amos 2:6–8, 3:9–10, 4:1–3, 5:7–15, 6:4–7, 8:4–7	In a series of prophecies spoken by Amos, God condemns the mistreatment of people who are poor and vulnerable, material greed, bribery, corruption, and the arrogance of wealthy people who ignore the human needs around them.
Amos 5:23–24	In this well-known quotation, God tells the Israelites: "Away with your noisy songs! I will not listen to the melodies of your harps. But if you would offer me holocausts, then let justice surge like water, and goodness like an unfailing stream."
Micah 2:1–3, 3:1–4	God condemns those who develop schemes to take other people's lands and leaders who do evil to their people.
Micah 4:1–7	In this optimistic prophecy from Micah, God promises a future in which he will bring justice and peace to the world's peoples.
Micah 6:8	In this inspirational quotation, Micah proclaims: "You have been told, O man, what is good, / and what the Lord requires of you: / Only to do the right and to love goodness, / and to walk humbly with your God."

Article 7 Social Teaching in the New Testament

synoptic Gospels
From the Greek for "seeing the whole together," the name given to the Gospels of Matthew, Mark, and Luke, because they are similar in style and content.

"I came so that they might have life and have it more abundantly" (John 10:10). What is the abundant life that Jesus talks about in the Gospel of John? Is he talking only about our resurrected life in Heaven? Is he talking only about our spiritual life? During his papacy, Saint John Paul II spoke about this passage:

> New life, the gift of the risen Lord, then spreads far and wide, flowing into every sphere of human experience: the family, the school, the workplace, everyday activities and leisure time.
>
> *That new life begins to flower here and now.* The sign of its presence and growth is love. . . . Life flourishes in the gift of self to others, in accordance with each person's vocation. . . so that all can share the gifts they have received, in a spirit of solidarity, especially with the poor and the needy.

The Two Great Commandments

Jesus summarized the New Law in his two Great Commandments, which are found in all three of the **synoptic Gospels**. This is how they appear in the Gospel of Mark:

> Jesus replied, "The first is this: 'Hear, O Israel! The Lord our God is Lord alone! You shall love the Lord your God with all your heart, with all your soul, with all your mind, and with all your strength.' The second is this: 'You shall love your neighbor as yourself.' There is no other commandment greater than these." (12:29–31)

The first Great Commandment places God at the center of our life. All of our thoughts, attitudes, and actions should flow from our love of God. As we have seen in previous articles, it is God's will that we treat every human life with ultimate respect, distribute the earth's resources fairly, and live in just societies. Further, the second Great Commandment emphasizes the social justice principle of the common good. If we truly love our neighbor as ourselves, we will take action to protect essential human rights and ensure that all people have what they need to live with dignity. Christ's Great Commandments are another foundation for the Church's commitment to social justice.

The person who is "begotten from above" thus becomes able to "see the kingdom" of God (cf. Jn 3:3), and to take part in building up social structures more worthy of every individual and of all humanity, in promoting and defending the culture of life against all threats of death. ("Message of the Holy Father Pope John Paul II for the VIII World Youth Day," 5)

While pope, Saint John Paul II taught us that Jesus' words mean that we need not wait until Heaven to know the abundant life. The new life we receive from Christ calls us to put love into practice through acts of charity and the building of just social structures. For he is not Lord of a Kingdom that begins in Heaven—his Kingdom is made present here and now through the Church, which is the seed and the beginning of his Kingdom on earth. This article highlights teachings from the New Testament that are foundational to the Christian's call to "take part in building up [just] social structures."

Jesus did not abolish the Old Law; rather his New Law has its foundation in the Old Law. The examples given in this article show how the New Law fulfills the Old Law so perfectly that the New Law reveals the Old Law's true meaning. Indeed because Jesus fulfilled the Old Law perfectly, he took upon himself all the sins against it and redeemed them, making salvation possible for all people. The social justice teachings of the New Law are one aspect of the fulfillment of the Old Law.

Teachings on Human Dignity

In teaching us about human dignity, Jesus started with the laws from the Old Law and commanded us to go beyond them. In the Sermon on the Mount, he says: "You have heard that it was said to your ancestors, 'You shall not kill; and whoever kills will be liable to judgment.' But I say to you, whoever is angry with his brother will be liable to judgment" (Matthew 5:21–22). A few verses later he says, "You have heard that it was said, 'An eye for an eye and a tooth for a tooth.' But I say to you, offer no resistance to one who is evil. When someone strikes you on [your] right cheek, turn the other one to him as well" (5:38–39).

Why would Jesus command these difficult things of his followers? The reason is because in these teachings he asks us to see other human beings from his divine perspective. Jesus sees his own image in every person and loves every person no matter how evil the acts he or she commits. He asks his followers to do the same. This is one of the most foundational principles of social justice: we must see the image of God in every human person and therefore must love all people as best we can, no exceptions allowed.

Seeing the image of God in other people is true even for our enemies. In the Sermon on the Mount, Jesus also says: "You have heard that it was said, 'You shall love your neighbor and hate your enemy.' But I say to you, love your enemies, and pray for those who persecute you, that you may be children of your heavenly Father, for he makes his sun rise on the bad and the good, and causes rain to fall on the just and the unjust" (Matthew 5:43–45). Jesus demonstrated this commitment to love his enemies by refusing to do harm to them, even when he was attacked, tortured, and killed. At his arrest, when one of his followers attacked those who had come for him, Jesus said: "Put your sword back into its sheath, for all who take the sword will perish by the sword. Do you think that I cannot call upon my Father and he will not provide [for] me?" (Matthew 26:52–53). And at his death, in a tremendous act of love, Jesus forgave those who crucified him, saying, "Father, forgive them, they know not what they do" (Luke 23:34). In the New Law, Jesus

Jesus' healing of the lepers reveals to us the dignity of all human beings. Who might be considered the lepers in our world?

© Brooklyn Museum/Corbis

teaches us that mercy and forgiveness are an essential part of God's justice.

Jesus also teaches us unconditional respect for human dignity by his love for people who were considered unimportant or who were societal outcasts. He spent time with and blessed the children his disciples tried to turn away (see Mark 10:13–15). He spent time with and even dined with public sinners, a practice that some religious leaders found shocking (see Luke 19:1–10). He touched lepers even though doing so made him ritually unclean (see Mark 1:40–42). He told parables about inviting "the poor and the crippled, the blind and the lame" to banquets (see Luke 14:16–24). Through these examples Jesus demonstrated the unconditional love and respect he expects us to have for every person, whether friend or enemy, celebrity or social outcast, religious or nonreligious, in the womb or at the end of life.

Teachings on Money and Material Possessions

Christ had a lot to say about money and material possessions; it was one of the topics he taught about most frequently. In the first beatitude Christ says, "Blessed are the poor in spirit, / for theirs is the kingdom of heaven" (Matthew 5:3). The Lukan version is more direct:

> Blessed are you who are poor,
> > for the kingdom of God is yours.
> Blessed are you who are now hungry,
> > for you will be satisfied.
>
> (6:20–21)

Jesus pairs this beatitude with a warning:

> But woe to you who are rich,
> > for you have received your consolation.
> But woe to you who are filled now,
> > for you will be hungry.
>
> (6:24–25)

Most of those listening to Jesus would have been shocked at this teaching. The common belief at the time was that wealth was a sign of God's favor and blessings. Jesus seems to be saying the exact opposite. Or more precisely, he is saying that detachment from wealth is necessary for entering the Kingdom of God. He makes this point even more clearly in later sections of the Sermon on the Mount:

> Do not store up for yourselves treasures on earth, where moth and decay destroy, and thieves break in and steal. But store up treasures in heaven, where neither moth nor decay destroy, nor thieves break in and steal. For where your treasure is, there also will your heart be. . . . No one can serve two masters. He will either hate one and love the other, or be devoted to one and despise the other. You cannot serve God and mammon [an Aramaic word meaning wealth or property]. (Matthew 6:19–21,24)

These teachings in the New Law continue the tradition of the Old Law when it comes to material possessions: the goods of the earth are meant for all people, not just a privileged few. Jesus even asked some of his wealthy followers to share their wealth with those who were poor. In his encounter with the rich young man, Jesus told him: "There is still one thing left for you: sell all that you have and distribute it to the poor, and you will have a treasure in heaven. Then come, follow me" (Luke 18:22).

The Acts of the Apostles and the letters of the New Testament give evidence that the early Church embraced the sharing of material possessions very seriously. Acts has this description of the practice of the first Christian community: "All who believed were together and had all things in common; they would sell their property and possessions and divide them among all according to each one's need" (2:44–45). And in the Second Letter to the Corinthians, Paul appealed to the Corinthians to

This painting is an artistic interpretation of mammon. Why do think the artist depicts mammon as a king? What do you believe the artist is trying to say through the presence, placement, and posture of the two other people?

be generous in helping another Christian community: "Your surplus at the present time should supply their needs, so that their surplus may also supply your needs, that there may be equality" (8:14).

Concern for the Poor and Vulnerable

Jesus' compassion for, and commitment to, those who are poor and vulnerable is well known. In a pattern you are now familiar with, he takes the teaching of the Old Law and intensifies it. The Old Law called the Israelites not to harm poor and vulnerable people and to minimally provide for their welfare. Now Jesus makes their care a requirement for entering the Kingdom of God. This is the message of the Last Judgment as told in Matthew 25:31–46. In this passage, those who care for people who are poor and vulnerable, as represented by the **corporal works of mercy,** are placed at God's right hand and receive the gift of eternal life. Those who do not care for people who are poor and vulnerable are placed at God's left hand and sent off to eternal punishment. The Parable of the Rich Man and Lazarus contains a similar warning (see Luke 16:19–31).

The Letter of James challenged the early Christian communities to be faithful in living out this commitment to care for those who are poor and vulnerable. The letter warns

corporal works of mercy

Charitable actions that respond to people's physical needs and show respect for human dignity. The traditional list of seven works includes feeding the hungry, giving drink to the thirsty, clothing the naked, sheltering the homeless, visiting the sick, visiting prisoners, and burying the dead.

Pray It!

A New Testament Prayer for Justice

Dear Jesus,
   Help me to respect the dignity of every person I meet,
      including my enemies and the people others turn away from.
   Help me to be poor in spirit,
      and share my material goods with people in need.
   Help me to take action to help the poor and vulnerable,
      and demonstrate my faith through my good works.
   You know it isn't easy to serve the needs of others,
      and to build a just society.
   So I ask to be filled with the power of the Holy Spirit,
      that I might become the just and peaceful person
      you call me to be.
   Amen.

social doctrine
The body of teaching by the Church on economic and social matters that includes moral judgments and demands for action in favor of those being harmed.

social encyclical
A teaching letter from the Pope to the members of the Church on topics of social justice, human rights, and peace.

against treating wealthy people with greater honor than poor people (see 2:1–9). It chastises people who say they have faith but who do nothing to help with the material needs of others: "What good is it, my brothers, if someone says he has faith but does not have works? Can that faith save him? If a brother or sister has nothing to wear and has no food for the day, and one of you says to them, 'Go in peace, keep warm, and eat well,' but you do not give them the necessities of the body, what good is it?" (2:14–16). The Acts of the Apostles recounts the appointment of seven men who were charged with caring for the widows (6:1–7). This appointment is regarded as the beginning of the diaconate. The New Law makes clear that action on behalf of those who are poor and vulnerable is a necessary requirement for being a follower of Christ. ✝

Article 8 The Social Doctrine of the Church: Papal Social Teaching

The eighteenth and nineteenth centuries (the 1700s and 1800s) were a time of dramatic change in the western world. In Europe and the United States, numerous scientific discoveries and applications led to new developments in navigation, medicine, communication, and manufacturing. These developments led to the rise of factories, an increase in international commerce, and the growth of ever larger cities with working-class populations.

At the same time, leading thinkers were also proposing new economic and political systems, such as capitalism, socialism, and popular democracies. There was a growing belief in society that the world's problems could be solved through the use of human reason and scientific understanding. This thinking had its roots in the Age of the Enlightenment, an eighteenth-century period in Western philosophy. During the Enlightenment some people rejected the belief that any truth could be known through Divine Revelation; they believed that all truth could be discovered solely through human reason. Unfortunately, this meant that some people also ceased to believe in the authority of the Church.

The developments resulted in big changes in governments and economics. Kings and queens were replaced with popularly elected parliaments and congresses. Agricultural economies were replaced by manufacturing economies.

Guilds and craftsmen were replaced with factories employing hundreds of people. Human society was changing in dramatic and fundamental ways, bringing new opportunities for human growth and development and new moral challenges. The Church responded by applying God's eternal moral truth to these new social challenges; the resulting body of teaching is called the **social doctrine** of the Church.

Factory conditions in the middle to late 1800s often dehumanized workers, treating them as a resource to be used, with little concern for their safety, comfort, or dignity.

On the Condition of Labor (Rerum Novarum)

In the middle to late 1800s, life in parts of Europe could be described only as completely miserable. In some countries the majority of people were unemployed and starving. Those with jobs were often little more than slaves, working seven days a week for wages that could barely put food on the table. Some factories were filled with children working in dangerous conditions for cruel supervisors.

In light of this social situation, Pope Leo XIII wrote the first of the modern **social encyclicals,** *On the Condition of Labor (Rerum Novarum)*, in 1891. In the opening of the encyclical, he states the conditions that he felt obligated to address:

© Bettmann/CORBIS

Catholic Wisdom

The Challenge of Transforming Social Realities

Transforming social realities with the power of the Gospel . . . has always been a challenge and it remains so today at the beginning of the third millennium of the Christian era. The proclamation of Jesus Christ, the "Good News" of salvation, love, justice, and peace, is not readily received in today's world, devastated as it is by wars, poverty and injustices. For this very reason the men and women of our day have greater need than ever of the Gospel: of the faith that saves, the hope that enlightens, of the charity that loves. (*Compendium of the Social Doctrine of the Church,* presentation page)

In any case we clearly see, and on this there is general agreement, that some opportune remedy must be found quickly for the misery and wretchedness pressing so unjustly on the majority of the working class: for the ancient workingmen's guilds were abolished in the last century, and no other protective organization took their place. Public institutions and the laws set aside the ancient religion. Hence, by degrees it has come to pass that working men have been surrendered, isolated and helpless, to the hardheartedness of employers and the greed of unchecked competition. The mischief has been increased by rapacious usury, which, although more than once condemned by the Church, is nevertheless, under a different guise, but with like injustice, still practiced by covetous and grasping men. To this must be added that the hiring of labor and the conduct of trade are concentrated in the hands of comparatively few; so that a small number of very rich men have been able to lay upon the teeming masses of the laboring poor a yoke little better than that of slavery itself. (3)

© Leonard de Selva/CORBIS

Recognizing the changing economic and political situation in the world, Pope Leo XIII wrote *On the Condition of Labor (Rerum Novarum)*, the first modern social encyclical, in 1891.

On the Condition of Labor was a groundbreaking document. It addressed these new social problems and made specific judgments about how to respond morally based on Divine Law. These are some of the important points this social encyclical makes:

- There must be cooperation between workers and business owners, and each must respect the rights of the other. Class warfare will not lead to a just and peaceful society.

- Workers have a right to work with dignity. Workers are owed a wage that can support families, reasonable work hours (including time off for Sundays and holidays), safe working conditions, and strict limits on child labor.

- Workers should be free to organize associations (now known as unions) to negotiate working conditions.

- Socialist answers that do away with all private property are false answers to these problems. People have a right to private property because it is the motivation for which people work. But workers and business owners must strive for a fair distribution of private property to avoid class warfare.

- The wealthy have a moral obligation to share their material wealth to alleviate the material needs of others, once their own basic needs have been met.

- Governments must serve the common good and make the protection of basic human rights (of all people and classes) their first priority.

On the Condition of Labor was a prophetic call to the people of the world to solve modern problems through reason and Divine Law. Though it can only be summarized here, it should be read in its entirety; you will find that it is still very relevant to today's world problems. It is online at the Vatican Web site.

Catholic Social Doctrine Documents

Since *On the Condition of Labor*, numerous papal and Vatican documents have added to the wealth of the Church's social doctrine. This chart lists many of these documents, with a few key points from each of them. Many of these are referred to in other articles. ✝

On the Condition of Labor (Rerum Novarum, 1891)

Pope Leo XIII

- addresses the Church's right to speak on social issues
- affirms that every person has basic rights that must be respected by society
- promotes the rights and just treatment of workers

subsidiarity
The moral principle that large organizations and governments should not take over responsibilities and decisions that can be carried out by individuals and local organizations, and that large corporations and governments have the responsibility to support the good of human beings, families, and local communities, which are the center and purpose of social life.

The Reconstruction of the Social Order (*Quadragesimo Anno*, 1931)
Pope Pius XI
- criticizes both capitalism and socialism
- criticizes the growing gap between those who are rich and those who are poor
- introduces the concept of **subsidiarity**

Christianity and Social Progress (*Mater et Magistra*, 1961)
Pope John XXIII
- shows concern for workers and women
- criticizes the gap between rich nations and poor nations
- says that excessive spending on weapons threatens society

Peace on Earth (*Pacem in Terris*, 1963)
Pope John XXIII
- warns against modern warfare, especially nuclear weapons
- says peace can be achieved only through a just social order
- gives a detailed list of the human rights necessary for a just social order

The Church in the Modern World (*Gaudium et Spes*, 1965)
Vatican Council II
- says the Church must serve the world and work with other organizations in promoting the common good
- condemns the use of weapons of mass destruction
- maintains that peace is not just the absence of war but is justice throughout society
- addresses many specific topics related to social justice

Brothers and Sisters to Us (1979)

The bishops have issued several letters on **racism,** but *Brothers and Sisters to Us* was their most comprehensive statement on the evils of racism. Here are some of the points they make in the letter:

- Racism is a sin because it violates the basic truth that all human beings have the same God-given dignity.
- Though some of the more obvious forms of racism have generally been eliminated from society, less obvious forms continue to exist.
- The letter also makes specific recommendations for Catholic churches and schools to support racial and ethnic diversity in the Church.

The Challenge of Peace: God's Promise and Our Response (1983) and Sowing Weapons of War (1995)

The Challenge of Peace: God's Promise and Our Response was written when the United States and the Soviet Union were at the peak of the nuclear arms race. The letter includes these points:

- Peace based on **deterrence** may be acceptable as an interim measure, but it is not a genuine peace and is not an acceptable long-term solution to the threat of nuclear war.
- Money spent on the nuclear arms race is money that cannot be used to help fight poverty and hunger.
- The nuclear arms race must end, the stockpiles of existing nuclear weapons must be reduced and eventually eliminated, and the creation of new nuclear weapons must be stopped.
- The bishops' letter *Sowing the Seeds of War* condemns the international arms trade as a scandal. The sale of weapons of war only for profit must be stopped. The letter makes the following points:
  o The United States must put its energies into building peace, not supplying arms.
  o The United States should lead the international effort to reduce and eliminate the use of landmines.

racism
Treating people of a different race without the full respect their equal dignity requires.

deterrence
The belief that war, especially nuclear war, can be prevented through the ability to respond to a military attack with a devastating counterattack.

Economic Justice for All: A Pastoral Letter on Catholic Social Teaching and the U.S. Economy (1986)

This letter is a comprehensive examination of economic justice in the United States, identifying good and bad aspects of the U.S. economic system. It echoes many of the themes in the papal documents on social justice, including the following:

- Economic decisions must be judged by how they protect or undermine human dignity.
- All members of society have an obligation to help those who are poor and vulnerable.
- The Church should be an example of economic justice in how she treats her employees, invests her savings, and serves people in need.

Confronting a Culture of Violence: A Catholic Framework for Action (1994), A Good Friday Appeal to End the Death Penalty (1999), and A Culture of Life and the Penalty of Death (2005)

The bishops of the United States have released a number of letters condemning violence in all its forms. A pastoral letter called *Confronting a Culture of Violence: A Catholic Framework for Action* was approved in 1994. This letter recognizes that the United States has higher rates of murder, assault, rape, and other violent crimes than many other countries. Some members of our society mistakenly turn to violence, especially abortion, to solve social problems. The bishops call Catholics to be leaders in confronting the culture of violence with Christ's message of peace.

Responding to Pope Saint John Paul II's teaching that the death penalty is rarely if ever needed to protect society, the bishops of the United States have repeatedly called for an end to the death penalty in the United States. In a Good Friday letter (1999), they repeat what they said in *Confronting a Culture of Violence*: "We cannot teach that killing is wrong by killing." Six years later, in 2005, they released a booklet called *A Culture of Life and the Penalty of Death*. The booklet calls for all Catholics to join the Catholic Campaign to End the Use of the Death Penalty.

^{Article}10 Defining Justice

Previous articles have explored the foundations for the social teaching of the Church found in Scripture and Tradition, teaching that has led to a rich understanding of the virtue of justice. The Catholic understanding of justice has many nuances and can become confusing at times. To help prevent this confusion, this article summarizes the different perspectives and definitions of *justice* used by the Church.

Magisterium
The Church's living teaching office, which consists of all bishops, in communion with the Pope, the Bishop of Rome.

Justice in the Bible

God originally created human beings to live in a state of justice. In their original state of justice, Adam and Eve were in good and loving relationships with God and with each other (also called right relationships, or righteousness). Thus, in the biblical vision, a just or righteous person is first in right relationship with God and second in right relationship with other human beings. The biblical understanding of justice reminds us that all justice flows from God and that human beings are called to participate in God's justice.

In the Old Law, justice is primarily about treating members of one's own community fairly and equally. For example, punishments are to be equal to the crimes, business practices must be honest, and the earth's resources are to be fairly

Live It!

Be an Informed Catholic

It is frequently said that the social teaching of the Catholic Church is her "best-kept secret." This expresses the frustration of those who believe that many people are not familiar with the Church's rich and specific teaching on social justice issues. For example, how many Catholics are aware that the Church supports the positive values of the free market but also warns against an unregulated free market that fails to protect human dignity? How many citizens are aware that the Church is opposed to the death penalty in the United States?

You can become an informed Catholic by reading the magisterial documents on social justice, which can easily be found on the Vatican's Web site or on the United States Conference of Catholic Bishops' Web site. Then you will have firsthand knowledge of the truth taught by the **Magisterium** and will better understand the Church's stance on challenging moral issues.

cardinal virtues
Based on the Latin word for "pivot," four virtues that are viewed as pivotal or essential for full Christian living: prudence, justice, fortitude, and temperance.

virtue
A habitual and firm disposition to do good.

justice
The cardinal virtue concerned with the rights and duties within relationships; the commitment, as well as the actions and attitudes that flow from the commitment, to ensure that all persons—particularly people who are poor and oppressed—receive what is due them.

distributed. In the New Law, the understanding of justice goes beyond fairness to one's immediate community. In the New Law of Christ, justice means extending God's compassion, forgiveness, and mercy to all people, even when that means sacrificing our own comfort and material wealth. Justice is one of the primary qualities of the Kingdom of God, and the Church is called to be a witness to, and an advocate for, justice on earth.

Justice as a Cardinal Virtue

As the Church's understanding of Divine Law has grown, she has added to her teaching about justice, noting that it is one of the four **cardinal virtues.** The cardinal virtues are human virtues—that is, **virtues** that we develop by our own effort with the help of God's grace. They guide our intellect and our will in controlling our passions and in making good moral choices based on reason and faith. The four cardinal virtues—prudence, justice, temperance, and fortitude—play a pivotal role in our moral lives. All other human virtues can be grouped around the cardinal virtues. As we develop the cardinal virtues in our lives, we become persons of moral character, meaning that we will do the right thing, even under difficult circumstances.

As a cardinal virtue, **justice** is the virtue concerned about the rights and duties within relationships and societies. It guides us in giving both God and neighbor what is their due and in working for the common good. Justice takes into account the needs of others as much as our own needs. It is about more than

© Scala/Art Resource, NY

This image depicts the cardinal virtues (the images in the four corners). What relation does the center image have with the cardinal virtues?

simple fairness; it asks us to bring God's compassionate and merciful love to those who are most in need. The virtue of justice recognizes that some people have greater physical and spiritual needs than others and require a greater sharing of material goods and spiritual support. It takes determination and dedication to be a person who lives the virtue of justice.

Classical Types of Justice

The Middle Ages saw the rise of Church-sponsored universities and the development of theology as an academic discipline. Great Church scholars like Peter Lombard, Bonaventure, Thomas Aquinas, and Duns Scotus developed comprehensive, systematic, and nuanced explanations of Church doctrine. Distinctions between commutative justice, legal justice, and distributive justice came out of their work. These distinctions continue to guide Church teaching on justice today. As you read the following descriptions about these types of justice, notice how they reflect the biblical understanding of justice.

commutative justice

This type of justice calls for fairness in agreements and contracts between individuals. It is an equal exchange of goods, money, or services.

© Stefano Bianchetti/Corbis

Commutative Justice

Commutative justice is the fairness that should exist when exchanging goods and services among individuals and institutions. For example, if you pay two dollars to buy a soda, you should get the full amount of the soda you purchased, not half a glass. On the other hand, the money you used to purchase it must be real dollars, not counterfeit money. Commutative justice requires that both parties receive exactly what they agreed to; in this way the human dignity of everyone involved in the exchange is protected. Commutative justice is the most fundamental form of justice in societies; without it all other forms of justice are impossible.

Saint Thomas Aquinas, pictured on the left, helped explain the distinctions between commutative, legal, and distributive justice. How would you describe each of these types of justice?

legal justice
The social responsibilities that citizens owe their country and society.

distributive justice
The responsibility that society has for safeguarding essential human rights and ensuring the just distribution of the earth's resources, with special regard for those people whose basic needs are going unmet.

Legal Justice

Legal justice concerns the responsibilities that individuals owe society. It is called legal justice because these responsibilities are usually spelled out in laws or other legal documents. Our country and community organizations cannot fulfill their responsibilities unless we fulfill our obligations to society. For example, we must obey just laws, pay our taxes, vote, and offer help in times of crisis. Legal justice requires us to fulfill these responsibilities to the best of our ability.

Distributive Justice

Distributive justice concerns the responsibilities that society has to its members. It is called distributive because it calls for the just distribution of the earth's resources to all people. In 1986 the United States Catholic bishops provided this explanation of distributive justice in *Economic Justice for All*: "*Distributive justice requires that the allocation of income, wealth, and power in society be evaluated in light of its effects on persons whose basic material needs are unmet*" (70). Thus the principle of distributive justice means, for example, that it is a social sin for people to go hungry in a country that can produce enough food for all its citizens.

Nations have a right and a responsibility to create and enforce laws safeguarding distributive justice. An example of this is laws that ensure that workers earn a livable wage and work in a safe environment.

Social Justice

Article 5, "Social Teaching in the Old Testament," mentions that the term *social justice* is a relatively recent addition to Church teaching. The term was needed to explain the teaching of the Church as it applies the virtue of justice to the complex reality of international politics, global economics, ecological dangers, and the horrific weapons of our time. The concept is introduced in the *Catechism of the Catholic Church*: "Society ensures social justice when it provides the conditions that allow associations or individuals to obtain what is their due, according to their nature and their vocation. Social justice is linked to the common good and the exercise of authority" (1928).

From this definition we can see that the primary responsibility for social justice rests with the institutions that make up society—that is, governments, businesses, and other civic organizations. But it is individuals who make the decisions that determine the policies and practices of these organizations. They are the leaders, or authorities, of these institutions. This is why the *Catechism* says that social justice is linked to the exercise of authority or leadership. Because in the United States and many other democratic countries citizens have a say in the country's decisions and policies, we all share some responsibility for ensuring social justice. ✝

The Saints on Justice

"The rule of justice is plain: namely, that a good man ought not to swerve from the truth, nor inflict any unjust loss on anyone, nor act in any way deceitfully or fraudulently." (Saint Ambrose of Milan)

"Let justice be done though the world perish." (Saint Augustine of Hippo)

"I beg you, remember this without fail, that not to share our own wealth with the poor is theft from the poor and deprivation of their means of life; we do not possess our own wealth but theirs." (Saint John Chrysostom)

Part Review

1. Describe four social justice themes that are present in the laws of the Old Testament.

2. What did the prophets proclaim related to social justice?

3. How does Jesus teach about unconditional respect for human dignity?

4. What are two New Testament passages that direct us to care for those who are poor and vulnerable?

5. What were the social realities that Pope Leo XIII addressed in *On the Condition of Labor (Rerum Novarum)*?

6. What three foundational principles is the social justice teaching of the Church built upon?

7. Which pastoral letter written by the U.S. bishops on social justice are you most interested in? Why?

8. Explain how the understanding of justice in the Bible is reflected in the three classical types of justice.

9. Define *social justice.*

world is a gift given by God for the good of all people, both now and in the future. People have a responsibility to care for their property and to use it to promote their own human dignity, the dignity of their families, and the dignity of all members of society. When some people have more property than they really need while others do not have even their survival needs met, society has a responsibility to encourage, and if necessary to require, those with more than they need to share with those who lack what they need to survive. ✝

The United States Bishops Speak

In a world where some speak mostly of "rights" and others mostly of "responsibilities," the Catholic tradition teaches that human dignity can be protected and a healthy community can be achieved only if human rights are protected and responsibilities are met. Therefore, every person has a fundamental right to life and a right to those things required for human decency. Corresponding to these rights are duties and responsibilities—to one another, to our families, and to the larger society. While public debate in our nation is often divided between those who focus on personal responsibility and those who focus on social responsibilities, our tradition insists that both are necessary.

(Sharing Catholic Social Teaching)

Article 14 Option for the Poor and Vulnerable

In previous articles we have seen how the Old Law, the New Law, and the social teaching of the Church all emphasize that individuals and society must have a special concern for people who are poor and vulnerable. This concern is rooted in the moral principle that Church teaching calls the **universal destination of goods.** This is the principle that the earth and all its goods belong to God, and he intends these goods to provide the things all human beings need to live with dignity. The universal destination of goods takes precedence even over the right to private property. This means no person has the right to keep accumulating money and possessions when other people lack the money and possessions needed for survival.

universal destination of goods

The principle that the earth and all its goods belong to God, and he intends these goods to provide the things all human beings need to live with dignity.

How does the social justice principle of option for the poor and vulnerable challenge a "me first" attitude? Why is it easy for many people to simply overlook the poor in their midst?

© shutterstock/jon le-bon

Why does God call humanity to place the needs of people who are poor and vulnerable first? Simply put, their need is greater. Choosing to defend people who are poor and vulnerable does not imply that they are necessarily better or more valuable than others; nor does it imply that people who are not poor are neglected by God, whose love does not exclude anyone. Society's call to place people who are poor and vulnerable first can be compared to the way parents pay special attention to a sick child. The parents do not love the sick child more than the other children, but they make the sick child their top priority because of that child's greater need.

The preferential option for the poor has two parts. First, it involves freely choosing to become friends or partners with those who are poor and taking on their problems as our problems. Christians are called to see Christ in all people, but especially in people who are poor and vulnerable (see Matthew 25:31–46). This is the choice to think of the poor as part of "us" rather than "those people." For those who are themselves poor or vulnerable, this choice means standing by other people in the same situation rather than trying to take advantage of them to get ahead. Unity with those who are poor and vulnerable is what the Church calls solidarity, a theme that is discussed in article 16, "Solidarity."

Second, the option for poor and vulnerable people means a commitment to take action to transform any injustices that prevent them from realizing their God-given dignity. If social policies or community attitudes prevent people from moving out of poverty or keep a certain group of people on the fringes of society, we need to advocate for change in those policies or attitudes. We need to become a "voice for the voiceless," a phrase that reminds us that people who are poor and vulnerable often have less access to society's decision makers, making it difficult for them to advocate for their own rights.

fair trade
An organized social movement and market-based approach that aims to help producers in developing countries to obtain living wages for their labor.

hutterstock/haak78

One way we can contribute to a more just society in our daily lives is to purchase fair trade products. Do you know where they are available in your community?

Live It!

Fair Trade

In developing countries small farmers are often fighting for survival because they are in a disadvantaged position when it comes to growing and selling their crops. For example, small farmers in countries like Guatemala are at the mercy of coffee buyers who set the prices large companies pay for coffee beans. Often the prices they will pay are not enough for the farmers to support their families. Because there is no competition among the coffee buyers, the small farmer has no choice but to accept the low price.

To live out the option for the poor and vulnerable, Catholics are responding to situations like the small coffee farmer in several ways. Catholic Relief Services (CRS) helps farmers in developing countries with training and equipment. Bishops in developed countries urge their governments to give preferential treatment to products coming from developing countries, and they encourage Catholics to participate in **fair trade,** which means purchasing goods from developing countries at a price that provides a living wage to the farmers and workers who produced them. Buying fair-trade goods requires the willingness only to pay a little more for our chocolate, tea, and coffee in order to help people in developing countries live dignified lives.

The Spiritually Poor

Material poverty is not the only form of poverty that we need to address. The Church also calls us to a special concern for those people who experience spiritual poverty. What is spiritual poverty? People who are spiritually poor lack a positive relationship with God, and they may also lack positive relationships with other people. Because of this their lives are often lonely and empty of meaning. They may experience isolation, depression, anxiety, and fear.

People who are spiritually poor can be materially rich or materially poor; spiritual poverty has many causes. Christians need to respond to people experiencing spiritual poverty with the love and compassion of Christ. We can help with our friendship and caring. We can show them how to have a relationship with God through prayer and the Sacraments. We can help them to develop the skills that are necessary to have healthy relationships with other people. And we can invite them to join the Body of Christ through participation in the life of the Church.

The Unites States Bishops Speak

In a world characterized by growing prosperity for some and pervasive poverty for others, Catholic teaching proclaims that a basic moral test is how our most vulnerable members are faring. In a society marred by deepening divisions between rich and poor, our tradition recalls the story of the Last Judgment (Mt 25:31–46) and instructs us to put the needs of the poor and vulnerable first.

(*Sharing Catholic Social Teaching*)

Article 15 Dignity of Work and the Rights of Workers

When we think about the value of work, we might think immediately of the amount of money we get paid for doing it or the things we can buy with the money we earn. Or if we are stockholders in a particular company, we might think about the value of work in terms of the profit the company will make and distribute to the stockholders if workers are productive. Catholic social teaching says, however, "The basis for determining the value of human work is . . . the fact that the one who is doing it is a person" (*On Human Work* [*Laborem Exercens*], 6). Work, and the economy in general, exists for the sake of people, not the other way around, and the value of work must first be measured by whether it promotes the human dignity of the worker.

God willed that human beings have the privilege of sharing in his work of creation. In Genesis God commanded the man and woman to "fill the earth and subdue it. Have dominion over the fish of the sea, the birds of the air, and all the living things that move on earth" (1:28). Pope Saint John Paul II interprets this passage for us:

> This description of creation, which we find in the very first chapter of the Book of Genesis, is also *in a sense the first "gospel of work."* For it shows what the dignity of work consists of: it teaches that man ought to imitate God, his Creator, in working, because man alone has the unique characteristic of likeness to God. Man ought to imitate God both in working and also in resting, since God himself wished to present his own creative activity under the form of *work and rest.* (*On Human Work*, 25)

"Man ought to imitate God both in working and also in resting, since God himself wished to present his own creative activity under the form of work and rest" (*On Human Work*, 25).

© Bettmann/CORBIS

Catholic Wisdom

The Redeeming Character of Work

At the end of his encyclical *On Human Work*, Blessed Pope John Paul II teaches that the toil of work is a result of Original Sin. But the toil of work can be a participation in the saving work of Christ:

> Sweat and toil, . . . present the Christian and everyone who is called to follow Christ with the possibility of sharing lovingly in the work that Christ came to do. This work of salvation came about through suffering and death on a Cross. By enduring the toil of work in union with Christ crucified for us, man in a way collaborates with the Son of God for the redemption of humanity. He shows himself a true disciple of Christ by carrying the cross in his turn every day in the activity that he is called upon to perform. (27)

© Ralf-Finn Hestoft/CORBIS

One of the rights recognized by the Church is the right of all workers to organize in order to advocate for fair salaries and just working conditions.

If human work is a sharing in God's work, then it stands to reason that human work has a sacred dignity that must be respected. This truth leads the Church to make the following moral conclusions:

- Human work should contribute to the increase of goodness in the world, not detract from it.
- Workers must be treated with dignity by other workers and by their employers.
- The rights of workers must be respected by business owners and protected by society.

Article 40, "Labor," presents a more complete discussion of the Church's teaching on these points.

From Soup Kitchen to Bakery Kitchen

A group of regular visitors to Haley House, a popular soup kitchen offering a variety of services for poor and homeless people in Boston, wanted to learn a trade so that they could find work. With financial help from the Catholic Campaign for Human Development, Haley House started training the people in bakery skills. The popular Bakery Training Program offers six months of paid instruction in basic baking and food service skills. And while they are learning the trade, the food and baked goods they create are sold at the Haley House Café and Catering business.

Dozens of the trainees have completed the bakery training program and have found work in the Boston area. According to Haley House's executive director, the food service industry typically pays a living wage and is one of the few industries open to people who may have a criminal

The United States Bishops Speak

In a marketplace where too often the quarterly bottom line takes precedence over the rights of workers, we believe that the economy must serve people, not the other way around. Work is more than a way to make a living; it is a form of continuing participation in God's creation. If the dignity of work is to be protected, then the basic rights of workers must be respected—the right to productive work, to decent and fair wages, to organize and join unions, to private property, and to economic initiative. Respecting these rights promotes an economy that protects human life, defends human rights, and advances the well-being of all.

(Sharing Catholic Social Teaching)

record. Haley House's Bakery Training Program is an excellent example of a program that teaches the dignity of work and supports the rights of workers. ✝

Article 16 Solidarity

Catholic social teaching says that a spirit of friendship and true community—between individuals, groups, and nations—is the basis for a just world. This is the Catholic social teaching theme of **solidarity.** While pope, Saint John Paul II defined *solidarity* as: "not a feeling of vague compassion or shallow distress at the misfortunes of so many people, both near and far. On the contrary, it is a firm and persevering determination to commit oneself to the **common good;** that is to say to the good of all and of each individual, because we are all really responsible for all" (*On Social Concern [Sollicitudo Rei Socialis]*, 38). Solidarity is based on the understanding that all people are part of the same human family, despite our national, racial, ethnic, economic, or ideological differences. Solidarity calls us to respect every person with the same respect we have for ourselves and that we respect the basic rights that flow from each person's inherent dignity.

When pope, Saint John Paul II saw the following things as signs of solidarity:

solidarity
Union of one's heart and mind with all people. Solidarity leads to the just distribution of material goods, creates bonds between opposing groups and nations, and leads to the spread of spiritual goods such as friendship and prayer.

common good
The good that is collectively shared by a number of people and that is beneficial for all members of a given community. Social conditions that allow for all citizens of the earth, individuals and families, to meet basic needs and achieve fulfillment promote the common good.

- when influential people who have a greater share of the earth's goods and common services feel responsible for weaker and more vulnerable people and share their goods with them
- when weaker and more vulnerable people renounce passive attitudes and destructive behaviors and actively "present their own needs and rights in the face of the inefficiency or corruption of the public authorities"
- when stronger and richer nations take moral responsibility for helping economically weaker nations
- when economically weaker nations are able to make their own contribution to the public good through the treasure of their culture

(Adapted from *On Social Concern*, 39)

The Solidarity movement in the 1980s and early 1990s in Poland embodied the Catholic social teaching theme of the same name. People in the movement worked together to promote their rights as workers and citizens.

© Peter Turnley/CORBIS

In the last century, it has become increasingly evident just how important the Christian virtue of solidarity is in creating a just and peaceful world. People are interconnected through technology, through business and financial practices, and through environmental concerns, to name just a few things. When one nation pollutes the oceans, many nations are affected. When one nation suffers an economic decline, people all over the world can be affected. Living in solidarity requires us to live in a way that doesn't deprive

others, near and far, of what they need to live. It also requires us to show a spiritual solidarity, a commitment to the principle that every person is a child of God, our spiritual brother or sister, no matter where in the world he or she lives. This kind of solidarity will grow only if Christians, empowered by the Holy Spirit, share the spiritual goods of faith that our heavenly Father has so graciously shared with us through his Son, Jesus Christ.

Defining the *Common Good*

Previous articles have referenced to the "common good," a concept that is tied closely to the theme of solidarity. The Church defines the *common good* as "the sum of those conditions of social life which allow social groups and their individual members relatively thorough and ready access to their own fulfillment" (*Pastoral Constitution on the Church in the Modern World* [*Gaudium et Spes,* 1965], 26). The common good requires these three essential elements:

1. A respect for the life and dignity of every person; the protection of each person's basic human rights.
2. A commitment to the social well-being and full development of every person, particularly by ensuring that all people have access to food, clothing, shelter, health care, education, work, family life, and so on.
3. The establishment of true peace, based in a just society, that provides stability and security for every person.

The United States Bishops Speak

Our culture is tempted to turn inward, becoming indifferent and sometimes isolationist in the face of international responsibilities. Catholic social teaching proclaims that we are our brothers' and sisters' keepers, wherever they live. We are one human family, whatever our national, racial, ethnic, economic, and ideological differences. Learning to practice the virtue of solidarity means learning that "loving our neighbor" has global dimensions in an interdependent world.

(Sharing Catholic Social Teaching)

stewardship
The careful and responsible management of someone or something that has been entrusted to a person's care. This includes responsibly using and caring for the gifts of creation that God has given us.

The principle of solidarity also means that every person is responsible for ensuring the common good. Before the invention of the radio and the airplane, the focus of an individual's concern for the common good was the local community and perhaps the people in his or her state or nation. Today, because of modern communication and transportation, the whole world is our neighbor. Thus Church social teaching emphasizes that the Gospel calls us to be concerned for the common good of people even in other nations and on other continents. ✝

Article

17 Care for God's Creation

This theme of Catholic social teaching is also rooted in the Creation accounts of the Book of Genesis. In the second Creation account, God placed Adam in the Garden of Eden "to cultivate and care for it" (Genesis 2:15), symbolically indicating the human responsibility to care for the earth. And in the first account of Creation, God commanded the man and woman to "Fill the earth and subdue it. Have dominion over the fish of the sea, the birds of the air, and all the living things that move on the earth" (1:28). Some have interpreted this command as permission to exploit the resources of the earth, as in domination. But the Church interprets this command as God's granting **stewardship** of creation to human beings. A steward is someone who takes care of a master's or employer's wealth and possessions, a serious responsibility. In a similar way, God commands human beings to care for his creation with love.

Renewable energy sources, such as windmills, are one way we can show greater care for God's creation.

© shutterstock/MaxFX

God created the earth to have a diversity of creatures each with its own goodness. Genesis portrays Creation originally as a world of interdependence, a world of order, because all its members—humans, animals, and elements— work together for the good of all. But through Original Sin, human beings disrupt the balance and harmony God intended. We now have the responsibility to participate in God's work to restore that harmony, even though sin continues to disrupt our relationship with creation. With God's grace at work through human beings, all creation is destined to give glory to God once again.

News reports constantly remind us of the ways human beings are negatively affecting creation: air pollution, water pollution, oil spills, factory farms, hunting animals to extinction, introducing invasive species of plants and animals, and using too much artificial fertilizer and too many pesticides.

Pray It!

Social Justice Examination of Conscience

This examination of conscience, based on the seven themes of Catholic social teaching, is adapted from an examination on the United States Conference of Catholic Bishops Web site:

- Do I respect the life and dignity of every human person from conception through natural death?
- Am I aware of problems facing my local community and involved in efforts to find solutions? Do I make my voice heard when needed?
- Do I live in material comfort and excess while remaining insensitive to the needs of others whose rights are unfulfilled?
- Do I urge those in power to implement programs and policies that give priority to the human dignity and rights of all, especially the vulnerable?
- As a worker, do I give my employer a fair day's work for my wages?
- Do my purchasing choices take into account the hands involved in the production of what I buy? When possible, do I buy products produced by workers whose rights and dignity were respected?
- Is solidarity incorporated into my prayer and spirituality? Do I lift up vulnerable people throughout the world in my prayer, or is it reserved for my personal concerns only?
- Do I litter? Live wastefully? Use energy too freely? Are there ways I could reduce consumption in my life?

The United States Bishops Speak

On a planet conflicted over environmental issues, the Catholic tradition insists that we show our respect for the Creator by our stewardship of creation. Care for the earth is not just an Earth Day slogan, it is a requirement of our faith. We are called to protect people and the planet, living our faith in relationship with all of God's creation. This environmental challenge has fundamental moral and ethical dimensions that cannot be ignored.

(Sharing Catholic Social Teaching)

But we should not forget the progress that has been made in fighting these threats to the earth in the last several generations. There are many challenges in caring for the earth and its creatures, but we also have had many successes that show God can work through us to make a difference if we act in solidarity.

Young People Are Stewards of the Earth

Teens are taking an active role in protecting the earth. Here are the results of a quick Internet investigation of environmental projects involving teens:

- Students in the Midwest test local lakes and rivers for pollution, including looking for genetic defects in frogs.
- Teens lead efforts to recycle used cell phones and ink cartridges.
- Young people speak out on the detrimental effects of artificial fertilizers and pesticides and urge their communities to support organic farming.
- Students in the San Francisco Bay area interview environmental experts and create news reports that they broadcast to other students through their school district radio.
- Middle school students in New England collect waste cooking oil from area restaurants, refine it into biofuel, and distribute it.

What actions by young people in your community can you add to this list? ✝

Part Review

1. Give three examples of how society can protect and defend the dignity of human life.

2. Why must the support and protection of the family have the highest priority in society?

3. What are the main categories of human rights outlined by Pope Saint John XXIII in his encyclical *Peace on Earth*?

4. Explain the moral principle of the universal destination of goods.

5. How does the value of work as understood by Catholic social teaching differ from the common societal understanding of the value of work?

6. What is solidarity? How are solidarity and justice related to peace?

7. What is the difference between exploiting creation and being a steward of creation?

Creating a Just Society

Part 1

Social Sin

For most of us, the idea of extreme poverty seems like a vague concept, but for millions of people in the world, it is an everyday reality. One billion of the world's people suffered from hunger in 2009; that's one out of every six people in the world. In 2008 three million children died of hunger and malnutrition before their fifth birthday. In 2005, the latest year for which this data is available, 1.4 billion people lived in extreme poverty, which means they lived on less than the equivalent of $1.25 a day (statistics from Bread for the World).

The truth is that these conditions do not need to exist. God created the world to have the resources human beings need to live free from hunger and material poverty. With rare exception, hunger, poverty, and homelessness are the consequence of human sins, sins that directly or indirectly cause an unjust distribution of the earth's resources. To make things worse, over time these human sins create social structures that support injustice and violence. People cooperate with these sinful social structures often without even realizing it.

Christ calls us to take action in response to suffering and injustice. In our globally connected world, this means not only responding to local needs but also responding to the needs of people around the globe. We do this by becoming aware of suffering and injustice, analyzing their causes, and taking appropriate action. Our response might take the form of direct aid to immediately alleviate people's suffering, or it might take the form of working to correct the social structures that led to the suffering and injustice. Both responses are needed.

The articles in this part address the following topics:

Article 18 The Social Side of Sin

sin

Any deliberate offense, in word, or deed, or desire, against the will of God. Sin wounds human nature and injures human solidarity.

natural law

The natural law expresses the original moral sense that God gave us that enables us to discern by our intellect and reason what is good and what is evil. It is rooted in our desire for God, and is our participation in his wisdom and goodness because we are created in his divine likeness.

mortal sin

An action so contrary to the will of God that it results in complete separation from God and his grace. As a consequence of that separation, the person is condemned to eternal death. For a sin to be a mortal sin, three conditions must be met: the act must involve grave matter, the person must have full knowledge of the evil of the act, and the person must give his or her full consent in committing the act.

Before we discuss social sin, let's quickly review what constitutes sin. **Sin** is an offense against God, a rebellion against his will and his desire that we live in loving communion with him and with each other. It is contrary to the obedience of Christ to the Father, and it is a rejection of God's love for us. When we sin, we put our will before God's will for us; we make ourselves more important than God.

Sin is also an offense against the truth of God's Eternal Law and against the gift of reason that we use to understand **natural law.** Sin leaves us wounded in body, mind, and soul and wounded in our relationships with God and others.

We can sin through our words, actions, or thoughts—not the thoughts that enter our heads unbidden and that we quickly dismiss, but the thoughts of revenge, lust, envy, or domination that we dwell upon and keep alive. In order to be sinful, a word, thought, or action must be deliberate; something that is truly accidental or unintended cannot be the cause of sin. Deliberately choosing to do something that is gravely contrary to God's Law is a **mortal sin.** This destroys the virtue of charity within us, which helps us to love God and our neighbor. Unless we repent of mortal sin, we cannot enter eternal life.

When judging whether a specific action, word, or thought is a sin, it is helpful to recall the three elements that determine the morality of any human act: (1) the object—that is, the specific thing the person is choosing to do, (2) the intention of the person doing the action, and (3) the circumstances surrounding the act. In determining whether a specific human act is morally good or morally bad, we must consider all three elements together. For a specific act to be morally good, both the object and the person's intention must be good. On the other hand, if either the object or the intention is morally bad, the specific act is sinful, even if something good results from it. For example, if we are generous toward someone not to be kind but to impress others, our generosity is not a morally good act, because the intention is selfish. Similarly, if we steal goods or money from others to help someone in need, the good result—helping another person—doesn't lessen the sinfulness of stealing. The circumstances play a secondary role, as they can affect the person's moral freedom or determine how good or bad the act actually is.

An Example of Sin's Social Impact

All sin has an impact on society. Sometimes this impact is easily seen; sometimes it takes some analysis to uncover its social impact. Let's consider price fixing as an example. Price fixing is an economic practice in which businesses that should be competitors all agree to charge the same price for a product or commodity. An example would be if all

© Marquette University Archives

Peter Maurin cofounded the Catholic Worker movement with Dorothy Day to help meet the needs of the poor and vulnerable.

Catholic Wisdom

The Dangers of Separating Religion from Society

Peter Maurin, the cofounder of the Catholic Worker movement, wrote a collection of short reflections on society and justice called *Easy Essays* (Steubenville, OH: Franciscan University Press, 1977). This is an excerpt from the essay titled "A Modern Pest."

> When religion
>> has nothing to do with education,
>> education is only information;
>> plenty of facts, but no understanding.
> When religion
>> has nothing to do with politics,
>> politics is only factionalism:
>> "Let's turn the rascals out so our good friends can get in."
> When religion
>> has nothing to do with business,
>> business is only commercialism:
>> "Let's get what we can while the getting is good."
>
> (Catholic Worker Web site)

the movie theaters in a city secretly agreed to charge fifteen dollars for a movie ticket. The motivation for price fixing is that the businesses involved don't have to lower their prices to compete with one another. They ensure a higher profit for themselves because the customers pay more. The problem is that this practice eliminates competitive pricing, a basic principle that free-market economies rely on to work fairly. This is why the United States and other countries have laws forbidding price fixing.

So let's imagine you are a recently hired executive in a company that buys corn from farmers and sells it to consumers. Your boss asks you to meet with executives from other companies that also buy and sell corn. Your assignment is to reach an agreement with the other companies' executives to sell corn at the same price—a high price that all the companies agree to. You realize that what your boss is asking you to do is price fixing, and it is a crime. However, he tells you that this is a common practice that has been going on for a long time. Reluctantly you agree to cooperate; after all, you are only following company policy and earning a living for your family.

Because you are following company policy, is your agreement to participate in price fixing a sin? And who is affected by your decision to follow company policy?

With a clear understanding of what constitutes sin, we conclude that price fixing is a sin, even if it follows company policy. Price fixing forces people to pay more than they should for a product because it eliminates the competition that should be part of a free market. It is essentially stealing, a sin against the Seventh Commandment. The act also disobeys a just law of society and therefore is a sin against the obedience to civil authorities called for by the Fourth Commandment. Therefore the object of the act itself is morally bad, making the act of price fixing a sin. A good intention, such as earning a living for your family, does not make this morally bad act morally right.

The Personal and Social Dimensions of Sin

Every sin has a personal dimension because every sin is the result of a real human person's making a free decision to disobey God's Law. Businesses do not commit sins; nor do governments or any other institution. It is true that sometimes sinful actions can become commonly accepted as ways of doing business or can even be supported by a nation's laws. This is discussed in article 19, "Structures of Sin and Social Sin." The sinful actions that result from unjust business practices or laws occur because one or more individuals have freely chosen to cooperate with such practices.

This personal dimension of sin means that every sin causes a spiritual wound in the person who commits it. This wound harms the person's communion with God, the source of his or her happiness. Until the person confesses the sin and is forgiven, the wound it causes will affect his or her spiritual health. This is why the Sacrament of Penance and Reconciliation is so important for living spiritually healthy lives.

Every sin, even when we think it doesn't hurt anyone, has a social dimension. Who is hurt by the sin of an unfaithful relationship? Who is hurt by someone cheating on a test?

shutterstock/Diego Cervo

All sin also has a social dimension. This is clear for sins such as murder and theft because of the immediate harm they cause other people. But what about sins that are private, seemingly affecting only the person or people who commit them? For example, the two people involved in an adulterous relationship might think that an act of adultery will not harm anyone else as long as no one finds out about it. But this kind of thinking is a denial of the real consequences of sin. For example, a person who commits adultery will experience guilt, be concerned about keeping her or his sin secret, and find it easier to commit adultery in the future. These things affect the person's ability to maintain an intimate relationship with her or his spouse, causing harm to the spouse even if the spouse never finds out about the adultery.

We accept that all sins have a social dimension. Even if some sinful actions do not cause immediate harm to someone else, they in some way affect the sinner's relationships with other people. This is because the spiritual wound caused by sin also harms our communion with other people, negatively affecting our relationships with them. As pope, Saint John Paul II said, "There is no sin, not even the most intimate and secret one, the most strictly individual one, that exclusively concerns the person committing it" (*Reconciliation and Penance*, 16).

The social effect of sin is not always immediately apparent. Whether the sin seems private, such as adultery, or occurs on a broader scale, it may take time for the social impact of some sins to take effect. Let's think about the person who thinks cooperation in price fixing isn't really harming anyone. The truth is that because of this sinful action, families are paying more for the product than they would have to pay if there were true competition in setting prices. If a family pays a dollar more a week because of price fixing, that adds up to $52 over a year's time. So over a year the price fixing is literally stealing $52 from a family—money

Cooperating with the Sin of Others

We can be responsible for sins that we do not personally commit if, by our actions, we support or participate in the sinful actions of other people. Sin with serious social consequences often requires this kind of sinful cooperation by many people. The *Catechism of the Catholic Church (CCC)* lists the following ways that people cooperate with other people's sins:

- by participating directly and voluntarily in them;
- by ordering, advising, praising, or approving them;
- by not disclosing or not hindering them when we have an obligation to do so;
- by protecting evil-doers.

(1868)

Can you think of a sin with serious social consequences that has been in the news recently? How did this sin involve the cooperation of other people?

that may mean doing without another necessity, especially for those living in poverty. Price fixing also causes harm to others involved in the buying and selling of goods. In the earlier example, the farmers who grow the corn are also not able to negotiate a fair price that covers their cost and allows them to earn a just wage.

Even though all sin has a social dimension, the social consequences of some sins, such as when businesses pay workers less than a living wage or when legislation is enacted to permit abortion, are much greater than those of other sins. The social justice teaching of the Church focuses on sinful actions like these. Confronting sin that has far-reaching social consequences requires an intentional response from Christians. Working for social justice requires persistent and coordinated social action to bring justice to the victims and to change unjust laws and practices. This is the focus of article 20, "The Circle of Social Action." ✝

structures of sin
Social structures that block justice and fail to protect human life and human rights. They are the result of the personal sin of individuals and in turn lead to personal sins.

Article 19 Structures of Sin and Social Sin

Could you be cooperating in someone's sin by buying tennis shoes or a soccer ball? This was a question in people's minds when a well-known company admitted that children living in Pakistan had made some of their products. The issue had come to light because some organizations committed to social justice had investigated the factories where the products were made. Company officials claimed they did not have direct knowledge that children were working in their factories to make their products, and they apologized that it had happened.

Some people said that an apology was not enough and stated that the company had a responsibility to establish procedures to guard against child labor and other injustices. This group of people and many others who learned about the company's practices also said that they would not buy the company's products until the company showed evidence that they had put such procedures in place to prevent this from happening again. These people were trying to change something that Catholic social teaching calls a **"structure of sin."**

Defining *Social Sin*

Catholic social teaching often uses the term ***social sin.*** The term can be confusing because it is used to describe several closely related realities. In his apostolic exhortation *Reconciliation and Penance,* Pope Saint John Paul II teaches us three correct ways of understanding social sin and one incorrect way of understanding it. The three correct understandings are as follows:

1. Social sin can be understood as the impact that our personal sin has on other people. This was discussed in article 18, "The Social Side of Sin." In the Pope's words, "With greater or lesser violence, with greater or lesser harm, every sin has repercussions on the entire ecclesial body and the whole human family . . . every sin can undoubtedly be considered as social sin" (16).

2. Social sin can be also understood as those sins that are a direct attack on another person or group's life, freedom, dignity, or human rights. In the Pope's words, "the term *social* applies to every sin against justice in interpersonal relationships, committed either by the individual against the community or by the community against the individual" (16).

3. Social sin can also be applied to the relationships that exist between communities of people. Whenever one group of people (for example, a social class, a nation, or an ethnic group) attacks the peace or freedom of another group of people, or treats the other group unjustly, this can be called a social sin. This is an analogical meaning because groups cannot really commit sins—only the individuals that are part of a group can do so. But the collective effect of many people's sins over time creates the structures of sin that are associated with particular groups.

Saint John Paul II goes on to say that the unacceptable way to define *social sin* is to contrast it with personal sin and to imply that somehow social sin is not the result of personal sin. Social sin is always the result of the personal sins of individuals, and each person must take responsibility for the effect his or her sinful choices play in sustaining social sin and cooperating with it.

Structures of Sin

In today's world many complex relationships are involved in producing the products we use every day. Take tennis shoes, for example. There is the relationship between the farmers who grow the cotton used in the shoe's fabric and the fabric manufacturers who buy the cotton from them. There is the relationship between the farmers who raise the

rubber trees and the rubber manufacturers. There is the relationship between the company making the shoes and the workers in their factories. There is the relationship between the company making the shoes and the governments that create and enforce the laws regulating working conditions, sales practices, and environmental protection. There is the relationship between the company manufacturing the shoes and the stores that sell the shoes. There are literally hundreds of people and social relationships involved in providing the shoes we wear every day.

The patterns of relationships that shape society, whether in business or in other networks, are known as

social sin
The impact that every personal sin has on other people; sin that directly attacks others' life, freedom, dignity, or rights; and the collective effect of many people's sins over time, which corrupts society and its institutions by creating "structures of sin."

social structures
The complex pattern of relationships that shape any society. They help determine how justice is lived out in society.

Fabric Manufacturers

Rubber Manufacturers

Farmers

Shoe Stores

Shoe Factories

© shutterstock/Ljupco Smokovski

social structures. The relationships needed to manufacture and sell something as common as a pair of tennis shoes illustrate the complexity of the social structures needed to provide the things we need to survive. Government, law, business, labor, education, families—all these are social structures too, because their existence is sustained and shaped by the relationships within and among them. Social structures shape and influence a great deal in our world, including who is rich and who is poor, who is fed and who is hungry, who has influence and who is overlooked, and even who lives and who dies.

A basic principle guiding social structures is found in the *Pastoral Constitution on the Church in the Modern World (Gaudium et Spes)*, a document of the Second Vatican Council. It says that our "social nature makes it evident that the progress of the human person and the advance of society itself hinge on one another. . . . The subject and the goal of all social institutions is and must be the human person" (25). This means that social structures should support and promote just and life-giving relationships. For example, companies buying rubber or any other crop should have policies that ensure that the producers they buy from are paid a fair price for their goods. Workers should have a shared attitude of hard work and honesty. Business owners should have a commitment to provide a safe place to work and to pay a just wage to their workers. The government should have regulations protecting workers from unsafe or unjust working conditions, the environment from damage, and consumers from poorly made or dangerous products and unjust pricing practices. These are some of the ways that social structures help to protect the common good.

When social sin goes unchecked, it can lead to horrendous atrocities such as the Holocaust. What modern atrocities can you identify that are a result of social sin?

© Reproduction/epa/Corbis

However, it is also possible for social structures to act as barriers to the common good. For example, workers might share an attitude that it's okay to steal company supplies for personal use. Or the owners of a business might have an unspoken policy of paying the lowest price possible for the manufacture of their goods, even if that means workers do not get paid a living wage. Or a country might have laws allowing people to discriminate against people because of their race or religion. The Church calls social structures that block justice and fail to protect human life and human rights "structures of sin." During his papacy, Saint John Paul II made four observations about structures of sin:

1. They are rooted in the personal sin of individuals. Structural sin does not just appear all by itself; it develops and grows because of the sinful choices of human beings.
2. They are the result of the interconnected choices of many people, not just one person.
3. Modern society avoids the terms *sin* and *structures of sin* in speaking of social structures. But we cannot correct unjust structures unless we think of them in ethical terms and challenge the personal sins that cause them.
4. The root causes of structures of sin are "on the one hand, the all-consuming desire for profit, and on the other, the thirst for power, with the intention of imposing one's will on others . . . at any price." In other words, selfishness is the basic attitude that builds and sustains structures of sin.

(Adapted and quoted from *On Social Concern [Sollicitudo Rei Socialis]*, 36–37)

People often view unjust social structures as permanent or unchangeable. Confronted by images of hungry and starving people, we might be tempted to say, "That's just the way the world works." But the social structures that shape society can be changed. Whether our social structures promote

Pray It!

Give Me a Just and Compassionate Heart

God of love and justice,
Give me a heart of compassion
    so that I am moved by the suffering of others.
Give me eyes that see as you see
    so that I can see the structures of sin that lead to social sin.
Give me a well-formed conscience
    so that I am honest about my cooperation with social sin.
Lord,
I am so sorry for my sin and the harm it has caused other people.
Forgive me, and strengthen me to love and serve others,
    rather than harm them or use them;
and strengthen me to work for justice,
    rather than to perpetuate injustice.
Amen.

greater justice or whether they act as barriers to justice is always the result of decisions made by individuals. And if individuals who have been supporting a structure of sin change and start making good moral choices, then a structure of sin will eventually change to a more just social structure. ✝

Article 20 The Circle of Social Action

A student wrote this moving reflection on the helplessness she felt while volunteering at a soup kitchen:

> There was a man there, I didn't catch his name, but he had an obvious mental problem. . . . There was no one there to help him, and probably no one who cared. It hurt to realize that I was sitting among society's forgotten. The people I read about every day at school and in the newspapers. I wanted to cry but I didn't, I couldn't, they didn't need my pity. They needed my actions, and I didn't know what to do. (James Youniss and Miranda Yates, *Community Service and Social Responsibility in Youth*, page 65)

The suffering caused by social sins and perpetuated through structures of sin is very real. Christ calls us to respond to our neighbor's needs and especially to those people with the greatest needs. Indeed he tells us that if we truly wish to be his followers, we must be aware of other people's suffering (see the Parable of Lazarus and the Rich Man, Luke 16:19–31) and respond to it (see the Parable of the Sheep and the Goats, Matthew 25:31–46). But like the student at the soup kitchen, many people do not have regular direct contact with poor or hungry people, and if they do, they do not know how to respond. Taking action requires us to be intentional in responding to the social needs of others. This article introduces an approach to taking social action called the circle of social action.

Awareness, Analysis, Action

In 1971, on the eightieth anniversary of the first social encyclical of the modern era, *On the Condition of Labor*, Pope Paul VI issued an apostolic letter titled *A Call to Action* (*Octogesima Adveniens*). The letter encourages Christians and all people of goodwill to continue their work for social

justice. Throughout *A Call to Action*, the Pope urges awareness of important social needs and social injustices, analysis
of the most appropriate responses to those needs and injustices, and most importantly, action to help meet those needs
and to correct injustices. These principles have inspired the
development of a concept that some people call the circle of
social action. People have developed elaborate explanations
of this concept, but the most straightforward explanation is
this: our faith calls us to be aware of social needs and injustices, awareness requires analysis, analysis results in action,
and action leads to deeper awareness and the circle begins
again. These three stages—awareness, analysis, and action—
are the circle of social action.

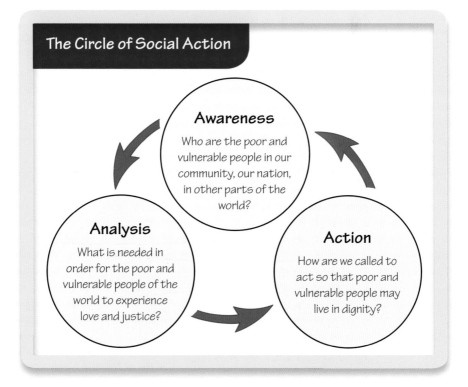

The Circle of Social Action

Awareness
Who are the poor and vulnerable people in our community, our nation, in other parts of the world?

Analysis
What is needed in order for the poor and vulnerable people of the world to experience love and justice?

Action
How are we called to act so that poor and vulnerable people may live in dignity?

Awareness

Before we can work for justice in the world, we must open
our eyes and our ears to the suffering of others. This may be
harder than it sounds. Many people are shielded from having
any regular contact with people who are poor, homeless,
jobless, sick, or suffering in any other way. How does this

happen? People with enough money buy homes in areas where there are no poor people. Social codes and civil laws keep homeless people off busy streets and out of affluent neighborhoods. In addition, the news media focus on stories that are new and sensational and rarely explore chronic social problems.

Because of these realities, each of us must take deliberate steps to raise our awareness of social needs and injustices. We can do this by volunteering with agencies and programs that serve people in need, such as soup kitchens, food pantries, Habitat for Humanity projects, and work camps. We can visit the impoverished areas of our cities, our country, or even other nations. We must find media sources that tell the real stories of people's needs and the social injustices that cause them. When we do these things, we will raise our awareness of our own personal responsibility to do *something*. Pope Paul VI reinforces this point in his letter: "It is too easy to throw back on others responsibility for injustice, if at the same time one does not realize how each one shares in it personally, and how personal conversion is needed first" (*A Call to Action*, 48).

Analysis

After becoming aware of the suffering caused by social injustice, we must be careful to avoid falling into two common traps. The first trap is that we are so overwhelmed by the problem that we become paralyzed into inaction. In other words, the problem seems so huge that we cannot imagine doing anything that would make a difference. The second trap is that we rush to do something without considering what the best course of action might be. In this case we could end up wasting our time or even making the problem worse. The way to avoid both of these traps is by taking time for analysis.

We can use two related sets of questions to help our analysis. First, we ask questions like these: What are the primary causes of this suffering and injustice? What sinful social structures support this injustice? What ways do I support or cooperate with these sinful social structures? Second, we ask questions like these: How can we bring God's love and justice to this situation? What personal action can I take immediately that will help in some way, however small?

Part 2

The Individual Person and Society

What is the world's best country to live in? In August 2010 *Newsweek* magazine devoted an issue to this topic. It considered five categories: physical health, education, economic competitiveness, quality of life, and political environment. It assigned scores for each of these categories to one hundred countries and averaged the scores together to create a single score for each country. Using this method the magazine determined that the world's best country to live in was Finland, followed by Switzerland and Sweden. Canada was ranked number seven and the United States number eleven.

The authors of the study acknowledged that this method isn't perfect and isn't the only way to measure a nation's quality of life. But the study raises an interesting question: What makes a country good? Catholic social teaching offers a real answer. A good country is one in which the individual citizens and the country's social institutions are committed to the common good. The common good is not just the responsibility of individual persons, nor is it just the responsibility of social institutions. If social institutions are not structured to support and protect the common good, those institutions could create structures of sin that could harm the people they should be serving. And if individual citizens do not support the work of social institutions, those institutions will fail to accomplish their purpose, and the common good will erode.

The articles in this part look at three important institutions that touch the lives of most human beings: the state, business institutions, and communications media.

The articles in this part address the following topics:

22 The Role of the State

state
Any organized political authority in a specific area; it can refer to city or county governments, state or regional governments, and national governments.

civil
Related to the state and its citizens.

Thomas Paine, one of the founding fathers of the United States, is reported to have said, "Government, even in its best state, is but a necessary evil; in its worst state, an intolerable one." This negative view of government is not shared by the Church. Some form of civil authority is required as part of God's plan, because human beings were created to live in community and human communities need organization in order to thrive. The *Compendium of the Social Doctrine of the Catholic Church* states:

> The responsibility for attaining the common good, besides falling to individual persons, belongs also to the State, since the common good is the reason that the political authority exists.[1] . . . The individual person, the family or intermediate groups are not able to achieve their full development by themselves for living a truly human life. Hence the necessity of political institutions, the purpose of which is to make available to persons the necessary material, cultural, moral and spiritual goods. (168)

The **state** has a necessary and positive role to play in God's plan of salvation. Though no state is perfect, throughout human history **civil** authority has made significant contributions to the common good (the exceptions are the morally corrupt governments that have emerged throughout history). Saint Paul recognizes this truth in his Letter to the Romans:

> Let every person be subordinate to the higher authorities, for there is no authority except from God, and those that exist have been established by God. Therefore, whoever resists authority opposes what God has appointed, and those who oppose it will bring judgment upon themselves. (13:1–2)

The higher authorities that Paul is talking about are civil authorities, and he is telling us that obedience to these authorities is also obedience to the will of God (unless the civil authorities are acting immorally).

Responsibilities of the State

Pope Saint John XXIII's encyclical *Peace on Earth* has a section specifically devoted to the relationship between individual

The "State" in Church Documents

Many Church documents use *state* to mean all levels of political authority: city and county governments, state governments, regional political authorities, and national governments. So when the word *state* appears in a Church document, it is referring not just to a state within a nation but to any level of government. This helps us to understand that the role and responsibilities of states as described in Catholic social teaching apply not just to nations but also to your city council and even the school board. Their purpose for existence is also to protect and promote the common good. A person who is the mayor of a small, rural town has the same moral responsibility for the citizens in his or her town that the president has for the citizens of the country.

In fact, the principle of subsidiarity requires that services are provided and laws are made at the lowest level of government that is practical. A higher civil authority should not take over the responsibility for things a lower civil authority can do just as well. For example, building codes should be made at the local or state level of government, as the requirements for building materials differ according to regional climates. Programs that provide housing for homeless and low-income people are also best provided at the local level. But laws regulating flying and airlines are best made at the national level, as the majority of flights travel between different states.

persons and civil authorities (see 46–79). In this section the Pope teaches that the primary reason for the existence of civil authorities is the achievement of the common good. A legitimate authority is committed to the common good of society and also acts morally in its work for the common good. The Pope makes clear that this does not mean protecting only what is good for some people; rather, "every civil authority must strive to promote the common good in the interest of all, without favoring any individual citizen or category of citizen" (56). He goes on to teach that the best way to protect the common good is for civil authorities to recognize, respect, defend, and promote the individual citizen's rights and to protect an individual's freedom to pursue these rights. These rights are summarized in article 13, "Responsibilities and Rights."

So how does the state make available the "material, cultural, moral and spiritual goods" needed for the common good? The state does this by actively creating "an overall climate in which the individual can both safeguard his own rights and fulfill his duties" (*Peace on Earth*, 63). And how does the state create this climate? Pope Saint John XXIII teaches that this climate is present when the necessary administrative, legislative, and judicial functions serve society and its citizens.

© shutterstock/Gary Blakeley

We are each called to be engaged in the political process to ensure that government promotes a "climate in which the individual can both safeguard his own rights and fulfill his duties" (*Peace on Earth*, 63).

Interestingly, these three functions correspond to the three branches of the government of the United States. Catholic social teaching recognizes that an effective civil authority must provide these essential services for the common good. The administrative, or executive, function sees that essential services such as "road-building, transportation, communications, drinking-water, housing, medical care, ample facilities for the practice of religion, and aids to recreation" are provided and regulated (*Peace on Earth*, 64). The legislative function provides laws to protect human rights and to ensure the harmonious functioning of society. And the judicial function ensures that laws are fairly enforced and that citizens have a legal way to correct injustices and protect their rights. These three functions ensure that the rights of individuals, families, and associations are protected and that they receive what is their due from the state.

As pope, Saint John XXIII also taught that states have an international responsibility to protect and promote the common good of all the people of the world, not just their own citizens. The concern of Christians and all people of goodwill must be larger than just their own national interests. We must be willing to be our brother and sister's keeper, even if that brother or sister lives on another continent. The Pope drives this point home:

> So, too, on the international level: some nations may have attained to a superior degree of scientific, cultural and economic development. But that does not entitle them to exert unjust political domination over other nations. It means that they have to make a greater contribution to the common cause of social progress.
>
> The fact is that no one can be by nature superior to his fellows, since all men are equally noble in natural dignity. And consequently there are no differences at all between political communities from the point of view of natural dignity. (*Peace on Earth*, 88–89)

the Nazis when the laws said the Jews were to be turned in. Civil rights activists like Martin Luther King Jr. landed in jail in Birmingham, Alabama, for refusing to honor laws that were racially prejudiced. Soldiers refuse to fight in wars that are not just. Medical personnel refuse to be part of teams that perform abortions. People gather for Mass and prayer even if religious gatherings have been banned.

Following your conscience and disobeying the commands of an immoral civil authority can be costly. Over the centuries thousands of Christian martyrs have given their lives to follow their consciences, speak out against injustices, and live out their faith. Thankfully, in democratic countries that protect religious freedom and that have legal checks and balances, there are fewer laws that require people to violate their conscience. But no civil authority is perfect. God calls

Why Shouldn't I Look Out for Number One?

It isn't uncommon to come across people who have this attitude: "I'm looking out for myself first because if I don't, no one else will. I don't have time to be worried about other people and their needs." These people have a point; each of us has a responsibility for our own physical and spiritual well-being. But it is a violation of God's will to ignore the welfare of society. Such a self-centered way of life is one of the effects of Original Sin. We were created by God to be "other-centered." As Jesus taught his disciples, "Whoever wishes to be great among you will be your servant; whoever wishes to be first among you will be the slave of all" (Mark 10:43–44).

There is a story related to this about a person who had a vision of Heaven and of hell. The people in hell were seated at tables filled with the most delicious food imaginable. But the only way they could feed themselves was by using spoons that were longer than their arms. They were starving because no matter how hard they tried, they could not get the food into their mouths. Now the vision of Heaven was exactly the same situation. But these people did not try to feed themselves; they fed one another. And behold, these saints were joyful and well fed.

It is difficult for some people to trust that caring for one another is the best way for each of us to have our needs met. Yet the sacred truth is that God cares for us continually through other people. We can see evidence of his care through the Church and through the love and concern of family, friends, and even strangers. When we share his love with others, we will find it returned to us many times over.

© Mark Peterson/CORBIS

In addition to voting, we can advocate for political change in other ways. When working for change, we should always act respectfully and peacefully.

us to recognize injustice, to refuse to participate in it, and to work to change it. ✝

^{Article}
24 The Church and the State

The Church and the state both have important roles to play in God's plan of salvation, roles that are complementary but distinct. Both seek to promote and defend the common good. However, the state's primary focus is the **temporal good,** which refers to the material needs that are part of earthly life. The Church's primary focus is the **spiritual good,** which refers to our need for God's grace so that we can be in communion with God in this life and for all eternity. The bishops of the Second Vatican Council defined the relationship in this way:

> The Church and the political community in their own fields are autonomous and independent from each other. Yet both, under different titles, are devoted to the personal and social vocation of the same men. The more that both foster sounder cooperation between themselves with due consideration for

the circumstances of time and place, the more effective will their service be exercised for the good of all. (*Pastoral Constitution on the Church in the Modern World* [*Gaudium et Spes*, 1965], 76)

Keeping the proper relationship between the Church and the state is very important. Our temporal good and our spiritual good are dependent on each other while here on earth, because our body and soul are inseparably united. So even though the state's primary focus is the temporal good of persons, it must also allow individuals and the Church the freedom to pursue the spiritual good. And even though the Church's primary focus is the spiritual good, it has a responsibility to promote and defend the temporal good when it concerns fundamental human rights or the salvation of souls. When the state and the Church are respectful toward one another, support each other's primary focus, and do not interfere with each other's primary work, the positive impact on the common good of all people is strengthened.

Autonomy and Independence

The Church has learned through experience that it is difficult to maintain her autonomy and independence in her relationship to the state. At times throughout history, civil authorities have tried to control the Church, and Church leaders have also tried to control the state. During the Middle Ages, some European kings believed that they should appoint bishops and even the Pope. On the other hand, during the same time period, some bishops and popes believed that they had the right to appoint or depose emperors and kings. This struggle over temporal and spiritual power led King Henry IV to invade Rome in AD 1081 with the intent to forcibly remove Pope Gregory VII.

temporal good
The aspect of the common good that focuses on the material and social needs that are part of earthly life.

spiritual good
The good that focuses on our need for God's grace so that we can be in full communion with God in this life and for all eternity.

King Henry IV invaded Rome when Pope Gregory VII decreed that King Henry IV should be deposed. Where in the world today do you see conflicts between the Church and secular governments?

© ANNEBICQUE BERNARD/CORBIS SYGMA

In China, the Communist party claims the authority to approve Catholic bishops. This has resulted in the formation of two Catholic Churches in China: the first, the Church led by bishops approved by the government; and the second, an **underground Church** led by bishops in union with Rome who have not been approved by the government. Although the preceding scenarios provide simplifications of complex historical situations, they illustrate the challenge of keeping Church and state separate and autonomous.

Christendom

The generally accepted dictionary definition of *Christendom* is "the collective body of Christians throughout the whole world." Or some people use the word as a descriptive term for the countries of the world in which Christianity is the dominant faith. There is nothing inherently wrong or dangerous with these definitions of *Christendom*.

A narrower definition promoted by some Christians can be considered dangerous, however. This definition understands Christendom as occurring when Christianity is the only officially recognized religious faith of a country. People promoting this understanding of Christendom want the country's political leaders to be appointed or approved by the Church, the country's laws and legal system to enforce Christian morality, only the Christian faith to be taught in schools, and so on. Ancient Rome came close to this reality after the Emperor Constantine converted to Christianity in AD 312 and legalized Christianity in the Roman Empire. Some European countries in the Middle Ages also practiced this concept. However, the Church should not be viewed in any way as a source of political leadership. Instead, the Church's mission is to protect the dignity of all people, and she does this by engaging in politics when human rights are threatened and the salvation of souls requires it. She carries out this work by means that are in accord with the Gospels.

The Church is opposed to becoming too closely identified with the state because this is not part of God's plan. If the Church is directly associated with political corruption or even political mistakes, her authority to preach the Gospel is compromised. The Church must remain free of political scandal so that her moral authority stays intact and she can be an uncompromised voice proclaiming God's truth to the world.

To maintain her independence from the state, the Church insists on having the following rights:

- the freedom to preach the Gospel and to evangelize (respecting the right of other faiths and religions to do the same)
- the freedom to provide public worship and administer the Sacraments
- the freedom to determine the Church's structure and organization
- the freedom to select, educate, and appoint its ministers
- the freedom to construct religious buildings and to acquire and manage the material goods necessary for the Church's ministry
- the freedom to develop associations for educational, cultural, health care, and other works of charity and justice

(Adapted from *Compendium*, 426)

The Church also recognizes her limits when it comes to political affairs. For this reason the Church does not align herself with any particular political party or political system. She takes positions on political issues only when there is a clear moral or religious principle at stake. With rare exception, bishops and priests do not run for, or hold, political office. By respecting these boundaries, the Church maintains her focus on the spiritual good and her prophetic role in promoting and defending issues of social justice.

underground Church
A term used to describe the Church when its gatherings are private and hidden from public view because of persecution or state laws forbidding religious practices.

How would you explain the role of the Church in politics to someone who believes that faith has no role in the political process because of the separation of Church and State?

© shutterstock/Konstantin L

© shutterstock/Avella

Catholic social teaching teaches that the exercise of religious freedom should be extended to all religions, not just to Catholicism and other Christian churches. The Church does not seek a political advantage over other religions; she trusts in God's truth to reach people's hearts through the power of the Holy Spirit. The Church also recognizes that if she were to be given political preference in some countries, she could easily be politically restricted or even banned in other countries. ✝

Article 25 Society and Economic Institutions

Have you ever thought about how big the U.S. economy is? According to the CIA's online publication The World Factbook, in 2009 the United States had a gross domestic product (GDP) of $14.26 trillion. The gross domestic product is the dollar value of all the goods and services produced in a country in a given year. If $14 trillion had been equally split among every U.S. citizen alive in that year, every man, woman, and child would have received over $46,000. If you were to split that amount among the entire world's population, every person in the world would receive over $2,300. That may not seem like much, but about 1 out 5 countries have a GDP that is $2,300 or less. Clearly economic institutions in the United States and other developed countries play a big role in developing a just society.

There are many different kinds of economic institutions: one-person businesses, family businesses, small- and medium-sized companies, nonprofit organizations, and huge national and multinational corporations (a corporation is a business that is recognized as a legal entity and whose existence is not dependent on any one individual). One might think that different moral laws would apply to these different institutions because of their vast differences in size and complexity, but the basic moral principles that govern rights and responsibilities of individuals and social groups apply to economic institutions of all sizes.

Regardless of their size and complexity, all economic institutions should serve the common good by producing goods and services that individual persons need to survive and thrive. This is their main role, but economic institutions also provide a number of other benefits to society. For example, the profit they make is often reinvested into new equipment, training, and research that improves efficiency, is beneficial to the environment, and results in new products and services. The wealth they produce is shared with owners, workers, and stockholders so they can purchase the goods and services they need. And economic institutions provide opportunities for individuals to use their time and personal gifts in service to the common good.

For these reasons, Catholic social teaching insists that businesses must be seen not only as a means of creating goods and services but also as human communities that must be attentive to the temporal and spiritual needs of the many people who interact with them: workers, managers, advisors, customers, and stockholders. Economic institutions do more than just make things; they help the personal and spiritual growth of people and society.

What are some examples of businesses that actively work to promote the common good? Are you aware of any local companies that are strongly committed to meeting the temporal and spiritual needs of their employees?

© shutterstock/Yuri Arcurs

Responsibilities of Economic Institutions

In light of their role in society, economic institutions have important social responsibilities. First and foremost, they have the responsibility to make sure their goods and services contribute to the good of society and not to its harm. For example, a company that distributes food nationwide can cause a national outbreak of illness because of salmonella poisoning or some other bacterial disease if it does not employ sanitary workplace practices. Or a toy manufacturer can cause infant deaths by creating toys with parts that can poison, choke, or suffocate a child. Preventing these types of dangers requires constant vigilance by the businesses and by civil authorities who have the responsibility for protecting society from dangerous and illegal practices.

Economic institutions sometimes bring harm to the common good through the products and services they sell. Pornography and prostitution are two obvious examples. Such products or services are sinful because their object is sinful. Less obvious examples might be the creation and manufacture of certain weapons of war that intentionally or unintentionally cause the disproportionate deaths of civilians. Catholic social teaching has challenged the use of nuclear weapons, biological weapons, and land mines because of this, a challenge that those who produce them must seriously consider. Economic institutions have a responsibility not to produce or distribute goods or services that are in themselves sinful, and they must not ask their employees to do anything immoral or illegal.

Businesses also have a responsibility to ensure that their manufacturing processes do not harm their workers or the environment. The United States has made great progress in the last several decades in ensuring worker safety and some progress in decreasing environmental pollution. Still there are businesses that periodically attempt to cut costs by not properly protecting their workers; mining accidents are frequently the result of this. And there is growing concern that modern farming practices are robbing the land of its fertility

Catholic Wisdom

We Work for Others and with Others

In the social encyclical *Hundredth Year* (*Centesimus Annus*), Pope Saint John Paul II discusses the social nature of work, a key principle in Catholic social teaching:

> By means of his work man commits himself, not only for his own sake but also for others and with others. Each person collaborates in the work of others and for their good. Man works in order to provide for the needs of his family, his community, his nation, and ultimately all humanity . . . in a progressively expanding chain of solidarity. (43)

and creating new strains of pesticide-resistant diseases and insects. Businesses must never stop examining their efforts to protect their workers and the environment. In order to promote justice and protect the common good, governments must create and enforce laws to protect workers and the environment.

Another responsibility of economic institutions is to charge fair prices for their products or services and to pay just wages to their employees. Business owners must not increase their own wealth by taking advantage of people's need for food, shelter, clothing, health care, and other goods necessary for a dignified life. Nor must they increase their own wealth by failing to provide their employees with fair wages and benefits. Catholic social teaching calls business owners and workers to be in respectful and just relationship, a topic covered more thoroughly in article 40, "Labor."

When economic institutions fail to meet their social responsibilities, the individuals responsible are committing sins against the Seventh Commandment, "You shall not steal." In the broadest sense, the Seventh Commandment forbids taking someone else's goods without the owner's permission. It forbids every way of unfairly taking or using something that is someone else's personal possession. It includes stealing people's health and safety, stealing the health of the environment (which belongs to all people), or stealing wealth from customers or employees through unjust pricing or wages. When this happens, commutative justice demands that the businesses involved make whatever **reparation** or **restitution** is called for.

reparation

Making amends for something one did wrong that caused harm to another person or led to loss.

restitution

Making things right with another person or people who have been harmed by an injustice, or returning or replacing what rightfully belongs to another.

The State and Economic Institutions

The state has an important role to play in relation to economic institutions. This role might best be characterized as similar to a referee's role in a sport's game. The referee makes sure the game is played fairly and calls foul when someone breaks the rules. Through its laws and regulatory agencies, the state makes sure businesses act morally and that they respect the free-market system (see article 41, "Economic Systems"). Thus governments have a responsibility to create and enforce laws protecting workers' safety. They have a responsibility to ensure that products (like toys and medications) are safe for citizens to use. They have a responsibility

© shutterstock/Kirill Livshitskiy

Through regulations, such as those applying to worker's safety and public health codes, governments work with businesses to protect the well-being of its citizens.

to ensure that small businesses can compete fairly with larger businesses.

Following the principle of subsidiarity, the government must not create its own businesses or overly regulate all aspects of economic life (just as referees do not play the game themselves or make calls about every aspect of players' interactions and techniques); rather, the state and economic institutions must work together to effectively promote the common good. This subject is given careful attention in the *Compendium of the Social Doctrine of the Catholic Church*:

It is necessary for the market [economic institutions] and the State to act in concert, one with the other, and to complement each other mutually. In fact, the free market can have a beneficial influence on the general public only when the State is organized in such a manner that it defines and gives direction to economic development, promoting the observation of fair and transparent rules.[2] (353) ✝

Slavery

When it comes to work and workers, we should be aware of one more social justice issue: slavery. Slavery still exists, and it exists because it provides some people with an economic advantage. Estimates indicate that every year, millions of people are forced into slavery across the globe. This slavery takes many forms. For example, people are forced into prostitution, or they are lured into another country and forced to work in prison-like conditions, sometimes even under the control of totalitarian governments that severely limit personal freedoms. The moral law condemns any act that leads to the enslavement of human beings—people bought, sold, or exchanged like merchandise. Immigrant workers, especially those without legal status, can be especially vulnerable to being exploited and even being made virtual slaves.

Article 26 Truth and the Media

How do you know when you are hearing the truth? We can certainly count on the media to communicate the truth to us, right? Unfortunately, the answer to that question is "not always." Major news networks sometimes carry stories without ensuring that all their facts are correct. The news on some networks is slanted to convey a particular political opinion. Some blogs and news stories change the meaning of a politician's speech by broadcasting or printing only selected parts of what he or she really said. And popular magazines often alter celebrities' photographs, making the celebrities seem more beautiful or perfect than they really are.

Catholic social teaching calls the media to be honest in communicating the truth; society has a right to this. A just and free society is built upon accurate and objective information. This becomes very clear in studying the use of propaganda throughout history. During the 1930s and through World War II, the National Socialist Party, commonly known as the Nazis, was ingenious in its misuse of the media. By offering misleading and biased information, the Nazis were able to win the loyalty of millions of Germans. This is but one example of the many that history provides us. In modern history, almost without fail, the groups involved in violent conflicts struggle to control the media. Once in control of the media, a group can begin communicating its own version of the truth to win the public over to its cause.

The immoral use of the media is a sin against the Eighth Commandment, "You shall not lie." God calls us to live in the light of truth and not in the darkness of lies, duplicity, and hypocrisy. We exercise the virtue of truth through the honesty of our actions and the truthfulness of our words. Lying consists of communicating something that

Freedom of speech means that we might encounter individuals or groups promoting a cause with which we disagree. Why is it important for the media to present information in an accurate and objective way, especially in these situations?

© Richard H. Cohen/Corbis

is not true with the intention of deceiving someone else. People involved in the creation and distribution of the media who knowingly communicate misleading information or distortions of the truth are committing a personal sin. And when this becomes a generally accepted practice, it creates a structure of sin. Sins against the truth, like all sins, require us to make reparation, or amends, for the harm we have caused. This includes working to change social structures that mislead or distort the truth.

The Purpose of the Media

Some governments and institutions control the information provided through the media. Why is the freedom of the media crucial for empowering citizens?

All social institutions should promote virtuous living; they must never be an obstacle to our moral life. They should promote the higher values such as honesty, forgiveness, compassion, and prayer over the lower values such as greed, selfishness, and revenge. Like other social institutions, the purpose of the media is to be at the service of the common good. When it is fulfilling its purpose, the media provides the information we need to make good moral choices by helping us to consider the personal and the social consequences of our choices. The media also provides a public forum where solutions to complex problems can be discussed in open and honest dialogue. But the media is called to do more than just provide information; it should also motivate and encourage the public to fulfill its social responsibilities.

© STR/Reuters/Corbis

In evaluating whether the media is fulfilling its purpose, the *Compendium of the Social Doctrine of the Catholic Church* asks this:

> The essential question is whether the current information system is contributing to the betterment of the human person; that is, does it make people more spiritually mature, more aware of the dignity of their humanity, more responsible or more open to others, in particular to the neediest and the weakest. (415)

In societies that place a high value on freedom of the press, such as the United States, the opportunity exists for the media to fulfill its role in God's plan. It is certainly true in these countries that media sources generally contribute to the betterment of humanity. Still there is room for these media sources to improve. What are the factors that impede the media's ability to fulfill its role in God's plan?

Challenges to Media Responsibility

Catholic social teaching mentions several impediments that affect the media's ability to provide accurate and unbiased information. The greatest impediment is when media sources cannot act freely. This can happen when another social institution, such as the state or a political group, controls the media sources. Or it can happen when a business or corporation has a monopoly on the media sources in a particular country or state. In these cases, media sources are often pressured to give biased information that benefits the state or the corporation that controls them.

Another impediment is financial concerns. In an attempt to make more money, media sources cover topics based on what will generate more viewer interest, thus bringing in more advertising revenue. This tends to lead to information that is biased or incomplete. For example, a news media source that is focused on making the most money possible may primarily cover disasters or acts of violence because more people are attracted to this sensational kind of news. This has led to the phrase "if it bleeds, it leads." The danger is that the public is then fed a constant media diet of "bad news" while the "good news," stories of hope and justice and positive action, goes unreported or underreported.

calumny

Ruining the reputation of another person by lying or spreading rumors. It is also called slander and is a sin against the Eighth Commandment.

detraction

Unnecessarily revealing something about another person that is true but is harmful to his or her reputation. It is a sin against the Eighth Commandment.

There is also the danger that the desire to create sensational news can lead to the sins of **detraction** and **calumny.** Detraction is making public someone's faults and failures without any valid or necessary reason for doing so. It is called detraction because it detracts from another person's good name. Even worse is telling a false story about someone in order to hurt their reputation. This kind of sin is called calumny, or slander. When detraction and slander occur in the media, the damage caused to a person's reputation can be almost impossible to repair.

Structural issues related to how people access the media can form another impediment to the dissemination of accurate and unbiased information. An example of this issue is related to the Internet. Many people now access media sources using the Internet, but in order to have the best access, people need a high-speed connection. In many cities and towns, subscribing to a high-speed connection can be costly, which means that many people who are poor will not have access

Using Information Media Critically

The average person is exposed to hours of media every day. This exposure has the potential to affect our attitudes and values, even unconsciously, which is why we have a responsibility to be disciplined and discerning in our use of media. Here are some suggestions for critically using information media:

- First, become informed. Many people do not even take this initial step, preferring to remain uninformed about important social concerns in their community and the world. Consciously or unconsciously, they may be thinking, "If I don't know about it, then I'm not responsible for doing anything about it."
- Though no news source is completely accurate or unbiased, seek out sources that try to be accurate and unbiased in reporting the news.
- When learning about an issue, study it from different perspectives. Check out multiple media sources. Listen to people who have different opinions, and apply reason and God's truth to their arguments. In prayer ask the Holy Spirit to guide you to the truth.
- Seek out information sources that are devoted to social justice concerns. The U.S. bishops' Web site has already been mentioned as a source of information, but many organizations devoted to social justice have regular newsletters you can read and subscribe to.

to one. On the other hand, high-speed Internet access is not even available in many rural areas because the cost of running the wires to provide the connection is so high. Situations like these can lead to a society in which some people are "information rich" and others are "information poor."

These impediments lead to structures of sin in regard to the media. These structures prevent the public from having access to socially responsible media sources and accurate information. The public must demand and support social structures that provide all people with access to the information we need to make good moral decisions as individuals and as a society. ✝

Part Review

1. What is the necessary and positive role the state plays in God's plan of salvation?

2. What responsibility do states have to other states? What is needed to help make this happen?

3. Name three civil responsibilities of citizens.

4. Define *conscientious objection.*

5. Why should the Church not be viewed as a source of political leadership? In what circumstances might the Church need to speak out on matters related to politics?

6. What role should economic institutions play in society? Why does the state have a role in the economy?

7. What are some of the social responsibilities held by economic institutions?

8. Why are honest and unbiased media sources important for society?

9. What are some impediments that affect the media's ability to provide accurate and unbiased information?

Respecting Human Life and Dignity

Part 1

Defending Human Life

The three parts of section 3 focus on respecting human life and dignity, a main theme of Catholic social teaching. This theme is rooted in the Fifth Commandment, "You shall not kill." The articles in section 1 and section 2 explore Catholic social teaching's fundamental principles; the articles in this section apply these principles to a variety of life issues. Part 1 discusses the protection of human life when it is most vulnerable: at its beginning and at its end. Part 2 discusses the threat of violence and war. Part 3 discusses prominent social issues that threaten human dignity.

All societies face a fundamental choice regarding the sanctity of life, a choice between becoming a "culture of life" a "culture of death." Societies that strive to be cultures of life work to respect and protect human life in all its stages, from conception to natural death. Societies in danger of becoming cultures of death fail to respect and protect human life in all its stages, denying important divine truths revealed through reason and Revelation. In many modern societies, such as the United States, the first victims of a shift toward a culture of death are often those people who are least able to defend themselves: the unborn, the infirm, and the elderly. Catholic social teaching calls us to challenge the culture of death and build a culture of life.

The articles in this part address the following topics:

- Article 27: A Culture of Life versus a Culture of Death (page 130)

- Article 28: Beginning-of-Life Issues (page 135)

- Article 29: End-of-Life Issues (page 141)

- Article 30: The Death Penalty (page 145)

27 A Culture of Life versus a Culture of Death

abortion
The deliberate termination of a pregnancy by killing the unborn child. It is a grave sin and a crime against human life.

euthanasia
A direct action, or a deliberate lack of action, that causes the death of a person who is handicapped, sick, or dying. Euthanasia is a violation of the Fifth Commandment.

During his papacy, Saint John Paul II issued the social encyclical *The Gospel of Life* (*Evangelium Vitae*) in 1995. The Pope was disturbed by moral shifts occurring in society. In some countries, sins against the sanctity of life, particularly **abortion** and **euthanasia,** were being legalized. In this encyclical he says it is as if there is a war against a fundamental moral principle, the principle that all human life is sacred:

> Today this proclamation [the sacredness of life] is especially pressing because of the extraordinary increase and gravity of threats to the life of individuals and peoples, especially where life is weak and defenseless. In addition to the ancient scourges of poverty, hunger, endemic diseases, violence and war, new threats are emerging on an alarmingly vast scale. . . . Unfortunately, this disturbing state of affairs, far from decreasing, is expanding: with the new prospects opened up by scientific and technological progress there arise new forms of attacks on the dignity of the human being. . . . We are confronted by an

Catholic Wisdom

Dishonoring the Creator

The Second Vatican Council document, *Pastoral Constitution on the Church in the Modern World* (*Gaudium et Spes*, 1965), has a powerful list of the sins against human life and dignity. How many of these deeds have you seen or read about during your years in high school?

> Furthermore, whatever is opposed to life itself, such as any type of murder, genocide, abortion, euthanasia or willful self-destruction, whatever violates the integrity of the human person, such as mutilation, torments inflicted on body or mind, attempts to coerce the will itself; whatever insults human dignity, such as subhuman living conditions, arbitrary imprisonment, deportation, slavery, prostitution, the selling of women and children; as well as disgraceful working conditions, where men are treated as mere tools for profit, rather than as free and responsible persons; all these things and others of their like are infamies indeed. They poison human society, but they do more harm to those who practice them than those who suffer from the injury. Moreover, they are supreme dishonor to the Creator. (27)

What are some reasons why these crimes against human life and human dignity cause more harm to those who practice them than to those who suffer from them?

even larger reality, which can be described as a veritable structure of sin. This reality is characterized by the emergence of a culture which denies solidarity and in many cases takes the form of a veritable "culture of death." This culture is actively fostered by powerful cultural, economic and political currents which encourage an idea of society excessively concerned with efficiency. Looking at the situation from this point of view, it is possible to speak in a certain sense of a war of the powerful against the weak. (3, 4, 12)

culture of life
A term used to describe a society that holds all life sacred, from conception to natural death. Such societies build social structures that protect and defend human life in all its stages.

In describing the current social reality, the Pope contrasts the **"culture of life"** with a **"culture of death."** A society that embraces a culture of life holds fast to the truth that all human life, from conception to natural death, is sacred. Such a society constantly works to build social structures that protect human life in all its stages. When a society denies that human life is sacred in all its stages, it is becoming a culture of death. Such a society creates structures of sin that allow human life to be attacked when it is most vulnerable.

© shutterstock/Monkey Business Images   © shutterstock/lev dolgachov   © shutterstock/Monkey Business Images

Culture of Life

Culture of Death

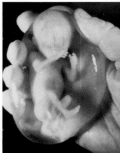

© shutterstock/Petr Nad   © www.Tamilnet.com/Handout/Reuters/Corbis   © Bettmann/CORBIS

culture of death
A term used to describe a society that does not hold human life sacred in all its stages. Such a society creates structures of sin that allow human life to be attacked when it is most vulnerable.

Some people believe that the highest social value is our right to pursue our personal goals and desires without any hindrances. How does this attitude contribute to the culture of death?

Causes of the Culture of Death

In *The Gospel of Life*, Pope Saint John Paul II identifies two contemporary causes of the culture of death. One cause is that many modern people embrace a distorted understanding of human freedom. This false understanding holds that all people should have the right to pursue their personal goals and desires without any hindrances. In this worldview, if something is an obstacle to pursuing your goals and desires, then you have the right, or even the obligation, to remove that thing from your life. The moral problem is that sometimes the "something" that people want to remove is life itself.

This understanding of freedom is false. Human freedom is a gift, not an absolute right. Because God created human beings in his image and likeness, we have been given the gift of freedom. The gift of freedom comes with responsibility: the responsibility to choose right over wrong, to choose love over hate, to choose solidarity over self-centeredness, to choose life over death. People who are exercising their freedom rightly would never choose an action that causes harm to another person to pursue their own personal desires.

The second cause of the culture of death is materialism. The Pope makes the point that when God is not the center of our lives, we often become preoccupied with material things, which leads to selfishness and the pursuit of pleasure as the primary goal of our lives. In his words:

> The only goal which counts is the pursuit of one's own material well-being. The so-called "quality of life" is interpreted primarily or exclusively as economic efficiency, inordinate consumerism, physical beauty and pleasure, to the neglect of the more profound dimensions—interpersonal, spiritual and religious—of existence. (*Gospel of Life*, 23)

When acquiring material things and pursuing personal pleasure are the highest values in a person's life, then suffering and sacrifice are things to be avoided. Because of this, a materialistic attitude leads to things like choosing our friends based on what they can do for us and making moral decisions based on what is easiest to do rather than what is truly right. We must be on guard against societal messages that encourage our self-centeredness rather than encourage us to trust in God.

Conscience and the Culture of Death

What particularly disturbs the Church—besides the number of deaths by abortion and euthanasia—is the erosion of personal **conscience** that underlies a culture of death:

> The end result of this [acceptance and legalization of sins against life] is tragic: not only is the fact of the destruction of so many human lives still to be born or in their final stage extremely grave and disturbing, but no less grave and disturbing is the fact that conscience itself, darkened as it were by such widespread conditioning, is finding it increasingly difficult to distinguish between good and evil in what concerns the basic value of human life. (*Gospel of Life*, 4)

We have recent historical examples of the erosion of personal conscience. On January 22, 1973, in its Roe v. Wade decision, the U.S. Supreme Court ruled that states cannot limit a woman's right to an abortion in any way during the first three months of her pregnancy. In effect, the decision has overturned state laws against abortion during all nine months of a woman's pregnancy, because the issue of the mother's health has come to be interpreted so broadly. Prior to the Roe v. Wade decision, however, the majority of U.S. citizens believed that abortion is wrong. Despite this deeply held belief, abortion was legalized because key decision makers wrongly believed that an embryo or a fetus is not a human person with the full rights of a person. The erosion of conscience in these key leaders was an important cause of the legalization of abortion.

Unfortunately, the legalization of a sin against human life results in a structure of sin that causes further erosion of conscience. After abortion became legal, more people began to accept the erroneous belief that unborn children do not have full human rights, and the number of abortions performed began to increase dramatically. But it gets worse. The legalization of abortion caused even more people to have an improperly formed conscience, which made it easier to accept other sins against human life. For example, a person might begin to think, consciously or unconsciously, "If it is okay to end the life of an unborn person because it is unwanted or inconvenient, isn't it okay to end the lives of other people who are unwanted or inconvenient?" Or another erroneous thought: "If we have the right to decide

conscience
The "interior voice," guided by human reason and Divine Law, that leads us to understand ourselves as responsible for our actions, and prompts us to do good and avoid evil. To make good judgments, one needs to have a well-formed conscience.

whether an unborn child gets to live or die, do we not also have the right to decide how that child is conceived?"

The erosion of conscience in regard to the sanctity of life is an important contributor to the culture of death. We must respect our conscience as a valuable gift for doing God's will. We are obliged to follow God's Law, to do good and avoid evil. God's Law makes itself known through our conscience. It is the judgment of reason by which we recognize the rightness or wrongness of a specific act. To build a culture of life, we must work to inform our conscience with God's Word as revealed in Scripture and Tradition, including Catholic social teaching. We must assimilate his Word in faith and prayer and put it into practice. A well-formed conscience will lead us to make the right moral judgment, in keeping with God's Commandments. It is principled, honest, and truthful. Because a well-formed conscience is so important

Promoting the Culture of Life

In the final section of *The Gospel of Life*, Pope Saint John Paul II turns his attention to how the Church must go about building a culture of life. Here are some of the main points:

- First and foremost, the Church must proclaim the Gospel of Jesus Christ. The Gospel message is a celebration of life, and if people believe in the Gospel, they will embrace the sanctity of life.

- In our prayer we must contemplate the wonder of life in all its richness and variety. In our worship we must celebrate the gift of life in praise and thanksgiving and by using the wealth of liturgical symbols present "in the traditions and customs of different cultures and peoples" (85).

- The members of the Church must serve others through works of charity. Through our service we help to bear the burdens of those who are suffering. Our service must be consistent to build the hope that comes from friendship and solidarity.

- Civil leaders have a particular responsibility "to make courageous choices in support of life, especially through legislative measures" (90). The Church recognizes that laws are not the only way to protect life, but they play an important role.

- Families play a special role in building a culture of life. Parents must lovingly accept each child that God gives to them. They must teach their children the gospel of life by witnessing to them respect for all people, a commitment to justice, generous service, and solidarity with people who are suffering and vulnerable.

to our moral lives, we have a serious obligation to educate our conscience well, and we must inform the conscience of society with the same seriousness. ✝

28 Beginning-of-Life Issues

In Saint John Paul II's encyclical *The Gospel of Life*, the Pope warns that in societies that are moving toward a culture of death, the lives of weak and defenseless people are particularly at risk. This has been tragically true in the United States. The National Right to Life Committee estimates that in the thirty-seven years between the Supreme Court's Roe v. Wade ruling and 2010, fifty-two million abortions were performed in the United States. This is a staggering number of innocent lives destroyed.

God wills every human being into existence in a unique, loving act of creation. He creates each person in his image and likeness. Therefore every person's life must be respected and protected, from the moment of conception until natural death, for every human being is sacred to God. The murder of any person, including the unborn, is a serious sin against human dignity and against the holiness of God. Building structures to protect the lives of the unborn is a necessary act of social justice in our time. This article addresses the sin of abortion and other moral issues concerning the beginning of human life.

Defining *Abortion*

Abortion is the deliberate termination of pregnancy by killing an unborn child in the womb. During the first eight to ten weeks of its development in the womb, the child is called an embryo; after that it is called a fetus. A number of medical procedures, some quite gruesome, are used to perform abortions. Scraping and suctioning the developing embryo from the mother's womb is the most common method. Sometimes a poisonous substance is injected into the womb, killing the embryo. Drugs have been recently developed—taken by the mother in the first few days

Pictures from inside the womb help us to realize how beautifully made human life is—from the moment of conception.

© shutterstock/Juan Gaertner

excommunication
A severe penalty that results from grave sin against Church law. The penalty is either imposed by a Church official or happens automatically as a result of the offense. An excommunicated person is not permitted to celebrate or receive the Sacraments.

after conception—that result in the death of the embryo. Further, methods of contraception have been developed to prevent pregnancy or to cause the demise of an early pregnancy.

Direct abortion—that is, abortion performed by any means to intentionally end a pregnancy and the life of an unborn child at any stage, interferes with God's plan for creation and destroys human life, and it is a grave sin. The woman having an abortion and the people who perform it are all guilty of a seriously evil act and subject to **excommunication.** An example of an indirect abortion is the rare case of a critically ill mother who requires a medical procedure that is not an abortion but that indirectly results in the death of her unborn child. In such a circumstance, an otherwise legitimate act also causes an effect one is normally morally obligated to avoid. This is known as the principle of double-effect and has its origin in Thomas Aquinas's teaching on homicidal self-defense. Under the principal of double-effect, the criteria for judging whether the harmful actions that result from the first action are morally tolerable are as follows:

- the original act is either good or morally neutrally
- the person committing the act intends the good effect of the act and not the ill effect that results from it either as a means to the good or as an end itself
- the good effect outweighs the bad effect, and the person carrying out the action exercises due diligence to minimize the harm

In the case of the indirect abortion that results from medical treatment needed to save the mother's life, the tragic situation would be morally tolerated because the death of the child is not directly intended.

Countering Arguments in Support of Abortion

Many of the arguments for abortion may seem reasonable at first glance but do not hold up under scrutiny. For example, some people argue that in the first weeks or months after conception, the embryo or fetus is not a human being. But modern biology, particularly the study of genetics, has conclusively shown this not to be true. Consider these medical facts:

- From the moment the sperm and ovum meet, the cell that they form has its own unique human DNA, different from that of any other human being. Left to its natural development, this cell will always develop into an adult human being, not a frog or a dog or a tree.

- The embryo's body is clearly differentiated from its mother's body. Although the mother's body provides oxygen and nourishment, as the embryo develops, it has its own intact and separate body. Its blood is not shared with the mother, and it often even has a different blood type.

- As early as twenty-one days after conception, the embryo's heart begins to beat. At nine weeks it has fingerprints. At twelve weeks the fetus sleeps, exercises, curls its toes, and opens and closes its mouth. At eighteen to twenty weeks, the fetus is fully capable of feeling pain.

These facts and others lead to one inevitable conclusion: A unique human life begins at the moment of conception.

Another argument people make in support of abortion is that a pregnant woman has the right to make choices about her own body, including the baby growing inside her womb. However, science provides clear proof that the baby's body, while dependent on the mother's body, is a distinct human being.

Some people also argue that if a baby's father abandons the unborn child and its mother, the woman should not have to carry the burden of having the child by herself. This argument is based on the false understanding of freedom discussed in the previous article, "A Culture of Life versus a Culture of Death." Freedom does not mean that we have the right to pursue our own well-being at the expense of someone else's life, including the life of the unborn. The answer to the problem of absent fathers is for society to make fathers accountable for the children they conceive and to be in solidarity with pregnant women by actively providing the support they need during pregnancy, childbirth, and beyond.

Defending the Unborn Person's Right to Life

Because abortion is a serious sin against the moral law, society has a responsibility to prevent this tragedy. We must work to change society's moral acceptance of abortion and overturn the laws that make it legal. Providing material, emotional, and spiritual help for women facing a crisis pregnancy can help to stop abortions. Encouraging people to see adoption as a loving alternative to abortion can help

artificial means of conception
The ability to create a new human life artificially, using means such as in vitro fertilization, artificial insemination, or surrogate parenting.

to save lives too. And greater respect for the gift of sexuality will prevent the situation in the first place.

The Catholic Church stands as a strong voice for those who cannot speak for themselves. Parishes, dioceses, and the national and state conferences of bishops, for example, foster respect for life by communicating the evil of abortion while finding ways to help women to avoid this tragedy. The Church actively reaches out to women who have had abortions to assist in their healing and reconciliation. If someone you know has had an abortion, only to realize later what a great wrong it was, programs like Project Rachel can help her to find healing and lead to reconciliation with God and the Church, especially through the Sacrament of Penance and Reconciliation.

Other Beginning-of-Life Moral Issues

Modern advances in genetics research have resulted in other beginning-of-life moral issues. One of these issues is using **artificial means of conception** to bring new human life into the world. One such artificial means is in vitro fertilization, which creates a fertilized ovum in a laboratory and then implants it in the woman's womb. Another means is artificial insemination, a fertility technique that artificially implants sperm in a woman's womb. A third artificial means is the use of surrogate motherhood—placing a fertilized ovum from one woman in another woman's womb and letting the baby grow inside her, usually to be given to the biological parents after birth.

As well-meaning as these techniques may be, they all share a serious moral flaw. The dignity of sexuality requires that children be created naturally. Children must be the outcome of the loving union of a husband and wife in sexual intercourse and not conceived through some artificial means of conception. Thus all three of these means of artificial conception are immoral. The Church, knowing that the pain of married couples who are unable to conceive children through natural means is very real, has great sympathy for husbands and wives who struggle with infertility. The Church encourages and supports research and medical treatments that increase the chances of natural conception for these couples. Nevertheless we must uphold

How would you explain the Church teaching on in vitro fertilization to a married couple who are considering using that technique to have a child?

© shutterstock/iDesign

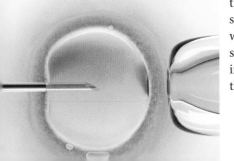

the dignity of sexuality within marriage through the creation of children as God intended.

Another beginning-of-life issue is prenatal testing, also called prenatal diagnosis, which involves testing the embryo or fetus for diseases or birth defects while the child is still in the womb. The Church teaches that prenatal testing is morally permissible as long as it does not cause any harm to the embryo or fetus and is done for the purposes of safeguarding and healing the developing baby in the womb or after birth. But prenatal testing for the purpose of deciding whether to abort the baby is morally wrong.

Genetic engineering, the manipulation of an ovum's or embryo's genetic coding, is yet another beginning-of-life issue. This could be used to produce a "designer baby," to create a person with predetermined qualities, such as a specific eye color, hair color, gender, and so on. Genetic engineering for this purpose is morally wrong because it falsely puts human beings into God's role of determining the uniqueness of every human person. However, certain forms of genetic engineering, called gene treatment or gene therapy, are used to prevent diseases or physical handicaps. These uses are morally permissible and encouraged as long as there is no significant possibility of harm to the fetus.

Another beginning-of-life issue, stem-cell research, has been a controversial political issue. Stem cells are unique

Cloning

Human cloning is the ability to create a biological reproduction of a human being who is genetically identical to the original person. Scientists have successfully cloned other mammals, such as sheep, but have not yet cloned a human being. Very likely the scientific ability to successfully clone a human being is close at hand. But should we clone humans?

The answer to this in Divine Law is a resounding no. There are several moral reasons why cloning a human being is an immoral act. First, as with other artificial means of conception, it separates conception from the true dignity that God intends for human procreation: the loving union of a husband and wife in sexual intercourse. Second, because human cloning is essentially the creation of human life in a laboratory or factory, it reduces human life to a commodity, something that can be planned, bought and sold, even owned. This is totally contrary to the sacred dignity of human life.

cells that have the potential to reproduce themselves as human tissues and organs. Stem-cell therapy is already used for bone marrow transplants and to treat leukemia. Scientists hope that it can be used to treat many other diseases and maybe even to grow new organs. However, one of the main sources for stem cells is fetal tissue, and some stem-cell researchers want to use aborted embryos and fetuses for their research. Though stem-cell research is not itself immoral—the Church, in fact, allows for research involving adult or umbilical cord stem cells—for obvious reasons the Church has condemned stem-cell research that uses aborted embryos and fetuses, as well as embryos created through in vitro fertilization. The good intention of stem-cell research does not justify the evil of abortion.

These beginning-of-life issues are clear examples of an important moral principle: Just because human beings have the technology and knowledge to accomplish certain actions does not mean those actions are morally right. Justice calls us to defend the rights of human beings from conception through all the stages of life. For that reason we must defend, care for, and heal the unborn as we would any other human being. ✞

Pray It!

Prayer for a Happy Death

The *Roman Missal*, the book of official prayers for the Mass, contains Mass prayers for a happy death. To pray for a happy death reminds us that our life on earth is only temporary and that we are preparing for our eternal and glorious life with God in Heaven. Keep this in mind as you pray this prayer based on the Mass prayers for a happy death:

O God,

who have created us in your image,

and willed that your Son should undergo death for our sake,

we humbly entreat your fatherly help

for the moment when we depart in death,

so that, overcoming the snares of the enemy,

we may be restored to life

in the embrace of your eternal glory.

We ask this through Christ our Lord. Amen.

Article 29 End-of-Life Issues

We now turn our attention to moral issues concerned with the end of our life on earth. In *The Gospel of Life*, Pope Saint John Paul II identifies the growing acceptance of euthanasia and suicide in developed countries as another sign of the rise of a culture of death. He wonders how people in countries that have promoted human dignity in so many other ways—reducing poverty, protecting worker's rights and women's rights, promoting racial tolerance, and so on—can so easily accept attacks on human life at its beginning and at its end. The Pope proposes this answer to the question:

> When he denies or neglects his fundamental relationship to God, man thinks he is his own rule and measure, with the right to demand that society should guarantee him the ways and means of deciding what to do with his life in full and complete autonomy. It is especially people in the developed countries who act in this way: they feel encouraged to do so also by the constant progress of medicine and its ever more advanced techniques. . . . In this context the temptation grows to have recourse to euthanasia, that is, to take control of death and bring it about before its time, "gently" ending one's own life or the life of others. In reality, what might seem logical and humane, when looked at more closely is seen to be senseless and inhumane. Here we are faced with one of the more alarming symptoms of the "culture of death," which is advancing above all in prosperous societies, marked by an attitude of excessive preoccupation with efficiency and which sees the growing number of elderly and disabled people as intolerable and too burdensome. (64)

This painting found in the Sistine Chapel depicts the Final Judgment. How does this painting remind us that death is the end of only our physical bodies?

As we consider these end-of-life issues, it is important to remember that death is only the end of lives for our physical bodies. Because our compassionate and loving Father sent his only Son for our eternal salvation, our souls live on, and we will know eternal life in resurrected bodies. In that life "He will wipe every tear from their eyes, and there shall be no more death or mourning, wailing or pain" (Revelation 21:4). If we focus on the promise of this ultimate destiny, we will more easily make the right moral choices at the end of life.

Euthanasia

The end-of-life issue that we probably hear about most frequently in the news is euthanasia, also called mercy killing. Euthanasia is a serious offense against the Fifth Commandment. God's Law makes clear that intentionally causing the death of a human being is murder, regardless of the motive or circumstance. The person choosing to die by euthanasia and the people helping him or her to do it are all guilty of a serious moral evil.

Proponents of euthanasia make it an issue of human freedom, saying that people who have a very serious physical handicap or people who are terminally ill and in severe pain—or their families, if the people are incapable of making their own decisions—have a right to choose to end their suffering. This sounds like a good and noble intention, but does it ever make euthanasia right? Remember the three elements that determine the morality of any human action: the object, the intention, and the circumstances. If either the object or the intention is bad, the action is a sin. In the case of euthanasia, the object, which is killing an innocent human being, is a violation of God's Law. It violates human dignity and the respect we owe to our Creator, the author of human life. Even the best of intentions—for example, sparing family members the anxiety of watching a loved one go through a long and painful disease, or easing a sick person's suffering—does not justify euthanasia.

When discussing euthanasia it is important to understand the Church's teaching on natural death. Rejecting euthanasia as a moral choice does not mean that we must use extraordinary measures to prolong the life of a person who is near death. When a person is near death, it is legitimate to reject extraordinary treatments such as heart pacemakers, special breathing apparatus, and medications whose only use is to prolong life. Likewise, the use of painkillers is allowed even if their use risks bringing death more quickly, because the direct intention is to relieve the dying person's suffering, not to cause his or her death.

To understand this shift, we need to remind ourselves of the New Law taught by Jesus. In particular we need to consider his teaching on mercy and forgiveness:

> You have heard that it was said, "An eye for an eye and a tooth for a tooth. "But I say to you, offer no resistance to one who is evil. When someone strikes you on [your] right cheek, turn the other one to him as well. (Matthew 5:38–39)

> You have heard that it was said, "You shall love your neighbor and hate your enemy." But I say to you, love your enemies, and pray for those who persecute you, that you may be children of your heavenly Father, for he makes his sun rise on the bad and the good, and causes rain to fall on the just and the unjust. (Matthew 5:43–45)

> Then Peter approaching asked him, "Lord, if my brother sins against me, how often must I forgive him? As many as seven times?" Jesus answered, "I say to you, not seven times but seventy-seven times." (Matthew 18:21–22)

Jesus did not deny the importance of the Old Law. It taught the Israelites to protect their community from evil and violent influences, and it limited the punishment that they could exact upon the people who broke the Law. But the Old Law was not complete. Jesus taught that divine mercy and forgiveness are more important than vengeance. Jesus completed the Old Law by teaching his followers to love all people and to hate no one, just as God—the Father, Son, and Holy Spirit—does. God did not change his mind about the death penalty; we just understand his will more fully because we have been given the New Law and the continuing inspiration of the Holy Spirit in our day. God's justice is rooted in mercy and love, not in punishment. He loves the most hardened sinner just as much as he loves the most perfect saint. If we are truly to follow God's Law, then we must be people who practice mercy

One form of capital punishment used in the United States is lethal injection. Why does the Church speak out strongly against capital punishment in our time?

© Mark Jenkinson/CORBIS

and forgiveness too, even toward those who commit the most heinous of crimes.

Another thing to consider in understanding the Church's teaching on the death penalty is the advancements we have made in criminal justice. The communities in Old Testament times did not have the capability to imprison people for a lifetime. To protect the common good, they had to execute dangerous criminals to keep them from hurting more innocent victims. This is not the situation in modern societies. The teaching of the *Catechism of the Catholic Church* recognizes this fact:

> If, however, non-lethal means are sufficient to defend and protect people's safety from the aggressor, authority will limit itself to such means, as these are more in keeping with the

Live It!

Examples of Forgiveness

Could you pray for someone who raped and killed a member of your family? Could you visit a murderer in prison and minister to the person? It is possible. The following people overcame their grief and desire for revenge. Find their stories online, and let them inspire you to be a person who practices the challenging work of forgiveness and reconciliation.

- Marietta Jaeger's youngest daughter was kidnapped while on a camping trip. A year later her daughter's kidnapper called to taunt her. Fighting her rage, Marietta expressed genuine concern for the man. Moved by her compassion for him, the kidnapper eventually opened up to her, revealing details that allowed the FBI to solve four murders, including Marietta's daughter's murder. Marietta remains committed to forgiveness and has since been an opponent of the death penalty.

- Thomas Ann Hines's son was killed by a young drug dealer who wasn't even given a life sentence. In her grief she was prepared to commit suicide, but something made her stop. She became involved in a prisoner rehabilitation program. Eventually she met with her son's killer, and after she heard the young man's story, her heart was moved with compassion. With the forgiveness she started to feel, her own emotional healing began.

- Bud Welch's daughter was killed along with 167 other people in the bombing of the Alfred P. Murrah Federal Building in Oklahoma City in 1995. Even though he had been a lifelong opponent of the death penalty, for months after the bombing he wanted to kill the bomber himself. But he worked through his feelings of grief and desire for revenge and began to advocate that the bomber not receive the death penalty.

concrete conditions of the common good and more in conformity with the dignity of the human person. (2267)

Building a culture of life requires society to respect all human life, even the life of murderers and terrorists. A culture of life is based in mercy and forgiveness. A culture of life gives even the worst criminal the chance to repent of his or her sin, return to God, and reform his or her life. Calling for an end to the death penalty is another way the Church calls our society to be a culture of life. ✝

Part Review

1. According to *The Gospel of Life*, what are two contemporary causes underlying a culture of death?

2. Explain the erosion of conscience that occurs in a culture of death.

3. Why is abortion a serious evil?

4. How would you answer someone who defends abortion by saying that a pregnant woman has the right to decide what to do with her body?

5. Define *euthanasia*.

6. Why doesn't a person have the right to choose when to end his or her life?

7. Why is the Church seeking to end the death penalty?

Part 2

Promoting Peace

If we need any evidence for the existence of Original Sin, we only have to consider the violence that human beings do to other human beings: humiliation, threats, rapes, beatings, torture, mutilation, and killing in ways too violent to imagine. Even though every major world religion discourages violence through its version of the Golden Rule, "Do to others as you would have them do to you" (Luke 6:31), human beings have an amazing ability to find reasons to ignore this wise advice.

Violent behavior is an offense against the Fifth Commandment, "You shall not kill." But most violence starts with small acts, not with murder or war. Small acts of violence have a tendency to escalate. The parties in a conflict keep retaliating with ever greater acts of violence; this is true for conflicts between individuals as well as conflicts between nations. These retaliations can eventually lead to murders and wars.

There is a justified use of violence, however. We, as individuals and as a society, have the right and even the obligation to defend ourselves and others from an unjustified attacker. In this circumstance we must use the minimum amount of violence necessary to protect ourselves and others.

Violence and wars are not inevitable. God calls us to confront social structures supporting violence and war and to build social structures that support nonviolent ways of resolving conflict. This is the Good News of the Gospel; Jesus Christ showed the world that there is an alternative to violence, which is found by practicing love, justice, forgiveness, and reconciliation.

The articles in this part address the following topics:

Article 31 The Causes of Violence

Let us start our exploration of the causes of violence by looking at U.S. murder statistics for 2009. The FBI received information on 13,636 murder victims in the United States for that year. Most of the victims were male (77 percent). An equal percentage of the victims were white (49 percent) and black (49 percent) despite the fact that only 13 percent of the population is black. Over two-thirds of the murder victims were killed by someone they knew (70 percent), and nearly a quarter were killed by someone in their own family (24 percent). Of the female victims, a significant percentage (35 percent) was killed by husbands or boyfriends. These murders occurred most often during arguments (41 percent).

When we analyze these statistics, it becomes clear that murder rarely occurs as a random act of **violence.** Why is it that human beings can bring themselves to the point of killing another person, especially someone they know and even profess to love? To understand this, we have to understand that the worst acts of violent behavior begin with lesser violent actions.

The Root Cause of Violence

To understand the roots of violence, we must first recognize that violence is more than physical assault and murder. Catholic social teaching defines *violence* as "any human action that causes harm to the life or dignity of another person." Thus an act of violence can be any psychological, social, spiritual, or physical attack on another person or persons. For example, all the following are acts of violence:

- calling another person a derogatory name
- **slandering** another person
- violating professional secrets, including the seal of confession
- **bullying** another person
- belittling another person by attacking his or her physical appearance, intelligence, ethnic background, family, religious beliefs, and so on
- manipulating or forcing someone into having sex against his or her will
- prohibiting someone from practicing his or her faith

violence
Any human action that causes harm to the life or dignity of another person.

slandering
Ruining the reputation of another person by lying or spreading rumors. Slander is also called calumny and is a sin against the Eighth Commandment.

bullying
Treating someone abusively, either verbally or physically, or forcing someone to do something against his or her will through violence or threats of violence.

spiral of violence

The tendency of violent acts to escalate as each party in a conflict responds to an injustice or an act of violence with an even greater act of violence.

- causing people to be poor, hungry, or illiterate because of the unjust distribution of the earth's resources
- selling weapons that will be used in immoral armed conflicts
- causing people illness or even death by tampering with the earth's environment

What do all these acts have in common? What are the underlying motives of the perpetrators of these acts of violence? All of these violent acts are rooted in negative feelings and attitudes in the heart of the perpetrator, attitudes such as selfishness, insecurity, greed, envy, and anger. These attitudes are the consequences of Original Sin. The *Catechism of the Catholic Church (CCC)* uses the example of the first murder in the Bible to explain this reality: "In the account of Abel's murder by his brother Cain [Genesis 4:1–16], Scripture reveals the presence of anger and envy in man, consequences of original sin, from the beginning of human history" (2259). The root cause of violence is the negative effect that Original Sin has on our attitudes toward ourselves and toward others.

We also know that there are many social causes that lead to violence. Poverty, oppression, discrimination, and other social sins make individuals and groups more prone to look for violent solutions to the problems that face them. When structures of sin make people's future look bleak and hopeless, they may feel that they have little to lose and much to gain by resorting to violent tactics.

Cain's murder of Abel reminds us that many acts of violence are rooted in negative feelings and attitudes such as greed, insecurity, and anger. What social conditions also lead to violence?

Still these factors don't explain how smaller acts of violence escalate into far more serious acts, such as murder, gang violence, terrorism, and war. A concept that can help us to understand how this happens is called the **spiral of violence.**

© Malcah Zeldis / Art Resource, NY

The Impact of Violent Media

We live in a culture marred by violence. Even if a young person never witnesses a murder in real life, she or he will probably witness hundreds of murders virtually. According to a 2009 paper of the Academy of Child and Adolescent Psychiatry, the "typical American child will view more than 200,000 acts of violence, including more than 16,000 murders before age 18." And if that child is a video game player, she or he will probably also commit hundreds of virtual killings playing first-person shooter games.

There is a growing consensus among health professionals that all of this virtual violence increases aggressive behaviors and desensitizes us to the pain and trauma caused by violent behavior. The U.S. Catholic bishops issued a statement in 1998 called *Renewing the Mind of the Media*. They said: "Rape, murder, torture, mutilation, and the gratuitous portrayal of these violent acts are among those things that deny the revealed meaning of our bodily existence and the respect due to the human body as God's creation. Portraying this kind of violence panders to what is senselessly destructive in our natures. As with pornography, in gratuitous portrayals of violence, persons are reduced to objects for the pleasure and profit of others."

© shutterstock/Yuri Arcurs

The bishops called for the government, the entertainment industry, citizens, and parents to be morally responsible in regulating, creating, and using media with explicit sexual and violent content. As a young person, you also have a responsibility for what feeds your mind, heart, and soul. Choose movies, music, and games that do not glorify violence and therefore do not endanger the formation of your conscience.

The Spiral of Violence

The spiral of violence is a concept that was used by Brazilian Archbishop Dom Hélder Câmara (1909–1999). Archbishop Câmara was known for his solidarity with the poor people in his country, and he wanted to explain to others how violence and injustice are related to each other. His concept is rooted in the human tendency toward retaliation and revenge. When one person is harmed by someone else, the typical response of the person who was harmed is to retaliate and hurt the other person in return. Now the original attacker has become a victim, and she or he responds by attacking the original victim with an even greater act of violence. Left unchecked, this spiral of violence grows in intensity and may grow to involve more people. Here is one way to describe it, along with an example of how it occurs in a personal relationship.

1. Basic Injustice

The spiral begins when people resolve a conflict selfishly, seeking only their own interests at the expense of the good of others. This results in some type of injustice. For our example, let's say a man promises to spend time with his fiancée on her birthday. But instead he chooses to go out with his friends without consulting her, leaving her to spend her birthday alone.

2. Violent Response

If the injustice is severe enough, it can prompt a response from those affected by it. People frustrated by injustice often see no other solution than the use of violence against their opponent. To continue our example, the next time the man and woman meet, she calls him a loser and an idiot and slaps him because she has been hurt by his unjust treatment of her.

3. Violent Counter-Response

Once one side decides to use violence to solve a conflict, the other side might see no other choice but to respond with an even greater violence. In our example, how do you think the man might react to his fiancée's name-calling?

4. Escalating Violence

The level of violence escalates as each side attempts to overcome the other with the use of greater force. Each side feels justified in its response because of the harm that has already been inflicted by the other side. When our hypothetical couple gets to this stage, the violence might escalate to physical violence, such as pushing, scratching, or slapping.

5. Violence Ends Temporarily, Followed by More Injustice

When one side finally uses enough force to overwhelm the other side, the conflict may appear to end. In reality, the spiral often returns to the first level, where the "winner" imposes his or her will on the "loser" in an unjust way. For example, imagine that the man slaps the woman hard enough to scare her. To avoid further violence, she tells him that she was wrong to criticize him for going out with his friends. He responds by telling her that she doesn't have the right to criticize his behavior and that she will get even worse treatment if she does it again.

THE SPIRAL OF VIOLENCE

Our example may seem crazy, and in a sense it is, because it is not based in reason, respect, or love. But situations like this happen every day, in every city across the world. And this example takes place between only two people. The same process is often at work in conflicts between people of different cultures, different tribes, and different nations. How do we stop this escalation of violence? There are two valid approaches to confronting violence in Catholic social teaching. One approach is to defend ourselves from an unjust attacker, using the minimal amount of force and violence if necessary. This is discussed in article 32, "War and Legitimate Self-Defense." The other approach is through nonviolent conflict resolution and nonviolent resistance to evil. This is discussed in article 35, "Nonviolent Resistance."

Pray It!

Prayer for Peace to Mary, the Light of Hope

Immaculate Heart of Mary,
help us to conquer the menace of evil,
which so easily takes root in the hearts of the people of today,
and whose immeasurable effects
already weigh down upon our modern world
and seem to block the paths toward the future.

From famine and war, deliver us.
From nuclear war, from incalculable self destruction, from every kind of war, deliver us.
From sins against human life from its very beginning, deliver us.
From hatred and from the demeaning of the dignity of the children of God, deliver us.
From readiness to trample on the commandments of God, deliver us.
From the loss of awareness of good and evil, deliver us.
From sins against the Holy Spirit, deliver us.

Accept, O Mother of Christ,
this cry laden with the sufferings of all individual human beings,
laden with the sufferings of whole societies.
Help us with the power of the Holy Spirit conquer all sin:
individual sin and the "sin of the world,"
sin in all its manifestations.
Let there be revealed once more in the history of the world
the infinite saving power of the redemption:
the power of the merciful love.

May it put a stop to evil.
May it transform consciences.
May your Immaculate Heart reveal for all the light of hope.
Amen.

(Pope Saint John Paul II, "The Message of Fatima," 1984)

The concept of the spiral of violence teaches us that the best way to confront violence is to address the issues that led to violence as early as possible. Christ calls us to refuse to participate in the spiral by choosing not to return violence for violence, hate for hate, and evil for evil. Jesus taught his disciples: "But to you who hear I say, love your enemies, do good to those who hate you, bless those who curse you, pray for those who mistreat you" (Luke 6:27–28). Saint Paul called the early Christians to respond in this way too: "Do not be conquered by evil but conquer evil with good" (Romans 12:21). ✝

Article 32 War and Legitimate Self-Defense

Let's be clear about this right from the start. Starting a war is an immoral act. It is a grave and serious sin against the Fifth Commandment. War and terrorism have been condemned by the Church's Magisterium throughout all of Catholic social teaching. "All citizens and all governments are obliged to work for the avoidance of war" (*CCC*, 2308). It is never an appropriate way to solve conflicts between people or nations, and it never will be. Pope Pius XII warned, "Nothing is lost by peace; everything is lost by war."

With the invention of nuclear, biological, and chemical weapons, modern warfare has the potential to cause death and destruction at a level never before seen in human history.

War has been one of the greatest threats to the sacredness of life throughout the millennia of human existence. Whether it is fought with spears and clubs or with nuclear weapons, the loss and devastation to human life is horrific. It is estimated that between forty million and seventy million people died as a direct result of the Second World War. You would think that would convince the world that we have to stop fighting wars but, as the sidebar "The Human Cost of War" shows, we have not learned that lesson.

© National Nuclear Security Admini/Science Faction/Corbis

Often wars cause more civilian deaths than soldier deaths due to the indiscriminate use of force, famines, diseases, and genocides that accompany the evil of war. One shudders to think of the devastation and death that would be caused by another worldwide war today through the use of nuclear, chemical, and biological weapons.

For these reasons the Church does everything within her power to prevent war from starting. Moral law requires that all citizens and all nations do everything they can to avoid war. Pope Paul VI, frustrated by modern warfare, affirmed this teaching when he called for "War no more; no more war!" in a speech to the United Nations assembly. Our reason and the Law of Love tell us that it makes more sense to resolve conflicts without using violence.

When war occurs we may be faced with an unfortunate reality. We may have to choose whether to defend ourselves through force and violence or through nonviolent resistance. Both approaches are part of the Christian tradition and supported in Catholic social teaching. The approach based in legitimate self-defense is covered in this article, and the approach based in nonviolent resistance is covered in article 35, "Nonviolent Resistance."

Legitimate Self-Defense

There are times when we may need to defend ourselves against an unjust aggressor. Divine Law does not forbid the use of legitimate self-defense. Our love for others, including our enemies, is balanced by our love for ourselves. Thus

Catholic Wisdom

The Church Condemns Violence

In this quotation from "Homily of His Holiness John Paul II" during a Mass in Drogheda, Ireland, Pope Saint John Paul II leaves no question about the Church's condemnation of the use of violence:

> I proclaim, with the conviction of my faith in Christ and with an awareness of my mission, that violence is evil, that violence is unacceptable as a solution to problems, that violence is unworthy of man. Violence is a lie, for it goes against the truth of our faith, the truth of our humanity. Violence destroys what it claims to defend: the dignity, the life, the freedom of human beings. (9)

when threatened with bodily harm by an unjust aggressor, we have a right to defend ourselves and other innocent people who are threatened by the aggressor.

> There are in fact situations in which values proposed by God's Law seem to involve a genuine paradox. This happens for example in the case of legitimate defense, in which the right to protect one's own life and the duty not to harm someone else's life are difficult to reconcile in practice. Certainly, the intrinsic value of life and the duty to love oneself no less than others are the basis of a true right to self-defense. (*Gospel of Life*, 55)

legitimate defense
The teaching that limited violence is morally acceptable in defending yourself or your nation from an attack.

But harming the aggressor must be a last resort. For example, if a burglar wants to steal from us, it is far better to allow the theft than to kill the thief. If we must fight to protect ourselves, our direct intention must always be to protect our own life, not to hurt or kill the aggressor. And we must use only the amount of force necessary to protect ourselves and other innocent people. Only if we have no alternative and have to kill or be killed is it permissible to kill in self-defense or in the defense of other innocent people. This principle is called the **legitimate defense** of life and is the basis of the right to self-defense.

The principle of legitimate defense also applies to defending innocent groups of people that are attacked by an unjust aggressor.

The men and women who serve in the military are called to protect the lives of the innocent, an act of legitimate self-defense.

> Legitimate defense can be not only a right but a grave duty for one who is responsible for the lives of others. The defense of the common good requires that an unjust aggressor be rendered unable to cause harm. For this reason, those who legitimately hold authority also have the right to use arms to repel aggressors against the civil community entrusted to their responsibility. (*CCC*, 2265)

For this reason the Church affirms those who serve in the military to protect the lives of innocents: "Those too who devote themselves to the military service of their country should regard themselves as the agents of security and freedom of peoples. As long as they fulfill this role properly, they are making a genuine contribution to the establishment of peace" (*Pastoral Constitution on the Church in the Modern World* [*Gaudium et Spes*, 1965], 79).

just war
War involves many evils, no matter the circumstances. For a war to be just, it must be declared by a lawful authority, there must be just cause and the right intention (such as self-defense), and weapons must be used in a way that protects the lives of innocent people.

conscientious objection
Refusal to join the military or take part in a war, based on moral or religious grounds. Conscientious objectors must seek official approval of their status from the government.

Just War

War must be a last resort whenever there is a conflict between nations. To help states to determine when war is justified, the Church has developed criteria that must be met for a war to be morally permissible. States that ignore or violate these criteria are committing unjustified acts of violence. The conditions for a **just war** are as follows:

- **Just cause** The state must have a just cause; that is, it must be using war to prevent or correct a grave, public evil.
- **Comparative justice** The good achieved through war must far outweigh the resulting loss of life and disruption to society.
- **Legitimate authority** Only duly constituted public authorities may use deadly force or wage war.
- **Probability of success** War may not be used in a futile cause or in a case where disproportionate measures—for example, using nuclear or biological weapons, resulting in massive loss of life—are required to achieve success.
- **Proportionality** The overall destruction expected from the use of force must be outweighed by the good to be achieved. In particular, the loss of civilian lives must be avoided at all costs.
- **Last resort** Force may be used only after all peaceful alternatives have been seriously tried and exhausted.

If any of these conditions are not met, the war cannot be considered just.

Catholic social teaching recognizes that legitimate authorities have the right to call citizens into military service for self-defense. For some Christians, answering this call and fighting in a just war fulfills a moral duty. Other Christians understand Christ's command to mean that they cannot, in conscience, fight in any war. The Church asks all governments not to force these conscientious objectors to serve as soldiers and to provide alternative ways for them to serve the needs of their country. (In 1971 the U.S. bishops issued *Declaration on Conscientious Objection and Selective Conscientious Objection,* calling on the United States government to allow selective **conscientious objection** so that a person serving in the military can legally refuse to fight in a war that he or she believes does not meet the criteria necessary for a just war. Currently, U.S. law does not allow military personnel this right.) ✝

so on—are a serious threat to peace. Their easy availability makes the possibility of regional conflicts and civil wars more likely. The driving motive behind the vast majority of the arms trade is profit. Arms dealers sell to the highest bidder, without any concern about their moral position. Often the same arms dealer will sell weapons to opposing sides of a conflict.

© STR/Reuters/Corbis

The Church's social teaching makes it clear that the production and sale of weapons are different from the production and sale of other goods or commodities. In fact, states have a moral responsibility to regulate the arms trade:

> It is indispensable and urgent that Governments adopt appropriate measures to control the production, stockpiling, sale and trafficking of such arms[1] in order to stop their growing proliferation, in large part among groups of combatants that are not part of the military force of a State. (*Compendium of the Social Doctrine of the Church*, 511) ✝

How is the production and sale of weapons different from the production and sale of other goods or commodities?

Article 34 Waging Peace

scandal
An action or attitude— or the failure to act— that leads another person into sin.

The promotion of peace in the world is an integral part of the Church's mission of continuing Christ's work of redemption on earth. In fact, the Church is, in Christ, a "'sacrament' or sign and instrument of peace in the world and for the world."[2] The promotion of true peace is an expression of Christian faith in the love that God has for every human being. (*Compendium of the Social Doctrine of the Church*, 516)

This quotation reminds us that peacemaking is an essential part of the Christian faith. In the Beatitudes, Christ teaches: "Blessed are the peacemakers, for they will be called children of God" (Matthew 5:9). God calls people of faith to be ambassadors of peace and reconciliation and to work for the development of just societies. Indeed, a Christian actively promoting violence in revenge or retaliation may be guilty of the sin of **scandal.** This article is called "Waging Peace" as a reminder that creating peaceful societies requires as much work, dedication, and sacrifice as fighting a war. We would be wise to remember that "winning" a conflict or a war, even a just war, is not a permanent solution to conflict. The spiral of violence is often only delayed; it has not been eliminated. True peace is the result of working at forgiveness, reconciliation, and justice; it is rooted in love, not hate.

Principles for Waging Peace

In answering Christ's call to be peacemakers, the Church asks us to keep the following three principles in mind:

The saving work of Jesus Christ ushers in God's Kingdom of peace. The human tendency to solve conflicts through violence is one of the consequences of Original Sin. With the redemption accomplished in and through Christ, humanity is no longer doomed to continue the spiral of violence. Even though we know peace only imperfectly in this life, we can be confident that God will bring the fulfillment of everlasting peace in Heaven.

Peace is a divine gift, a fruit of the Holy Spirit, given to those who place their faith in Jesus Christ: "Peace I leave with you; my peace I give to you. Not as the world gives do I give it to you. Do not let your hearts be troubled or

afraid" (John 14:27). Through our participation in the life of the Church, particularly through the Sacrament of the Eucharist and the Sacrament of Penance and Reconciliation, we receive the grace of knowing God's peace in our inner lives, even though conflict and violence may be all around us.

Peace is more than just the absence of violence. The word that Jesus used for "peace" was *salaam* (Arabic) or *shalom* (Hebrew). *Shalom* is used as a greeting, but it is also a blessing. It means more than just wishing that a person has peace in his or her life. *Shalom* means that you also desire that the person has just, loving relationships with God and with other people. A happy and peaceful life is built on this foundation. The concept of *shalom* helps us to understand that our work for peace is not focused on ending conflict only; we can end conflicts by ignoring them, by passively accepting an injustice, or by overpowering our opponent. But none of these ways leads to true peace. True peace requires building loving and just relationships among individuals and societal groups.

Being a peacemaker is not easy, but it is something Christ calls each of us to be. What is one way you can be a peacemaker in your family, school, or community starting today?

Waging Peace through Love

If we wish to have peaceful societies, then we must not wait until violence and war break out before we start working for peace. So what are some concrete ways we can answer the call to be peacemakers? Catholic social teaching suggests the following strategies. As you read them, think of how each of these strategies is also an act of love.

Loving Your Attacker: A True Story

What would you *do* if a stranger kicked in your bedroom door in the middle of the night? Angie O'Gormon, a dedicated Christian peacemaker, describes in her article "Defense through Disarmament," how she defused a very personally dangerous situation with love. Angie was sleeping in her home when she was awakened by a noise. She describes what happened next:

> He was verbally abusive as he walked over to my bed. As I lay there, feeling a fear and vulnerability that I had never experienced, several thoughts ran through my head. The first was the uselessness of screaming. The second was the fallacy of thinking safety depends on having a gun hidden under your pillow. Somehow I could not imagine this man standing patiently while I reached under my pillow for a gun. The third thought, I believe, saved my life. I realized with a certain clarity that either he and I made it through this situation safely—together—or we would both be damaged. . . . That thought did not free me from feelings of fear but from fear's control over my ability to respond. I found myself acting out of concern for both our safety. . . . (pages 242–243)

Angie started talking to the man about the time, how he got in, about how she didn't have the money to repair the door he broke. He started talking about his own problems. "We talked until we were no longer strangers and I felt it was safe to ask him to leave," she said. When he refused she offered to let him sleep downstairs. "He went downstairs, and I sat in bed, wide awake and shaking for the rest of the night. The next morning we ate breakfast together and he left."

Because of Angie's faith and her long-term commitment to loving nonviolence, she was spiritually prepared to react with love in a potentially violent situation. She did not respond as a victim, and she could see her attacker as a human being in trouble. She surprised him by showing him her humanity and expressing concern for his. In that moment of surprise, he reconsidered his actions, and the spiral of violence was broken. This will not happen every time we try to break the spiral of violence, but it will never happen if we do not try.

Complete Commitment to Nonviolence

Many Christians have committed to resisting evil through love only, even rejecting the right to legitimate defense. They believe that Christ calls them to resist evil always with love, never with violence. These Christians are even willing to die rather than commit an act of violence against another person. They will not fight in the military, even in a just war. In their document *The Challenge of Peace*, the U.S. bishops recognize the sacrifice of soldiers who have laid down their lives in the legitimate defense of others as one way of fighting for peace. But they also recognize the witness of those Christians committed to **nonviolent resistance** as another way that God calls Christians to be peacemakers:

**nonviolent
resistance**
To confront injustice
and violence with love,
using only nonviolent
strategies in working
for justice and peace.

> We see many deeply sincere individuals who, far from being indifferent or apathetic to world evils, believe strongly in conscience that they are best defending true peace by refusing to bear arms. In some cases they are motivated by their understanding of the gospel and the life and death of Jesus as forbidding all violence. In others, their motivation is simply to give personal example of Christian forbearance as a positive, constructive approach toward loving reconciliation with enemies. In still other cases, they propose or engage in "active non-violence" as programmed resistance to thwart aggression, or to render ineffective any oppression attempted by force of arms. No government, and certainly no Christian, may simply assume that such individuals are mere pawns of conspiratorial forces or guilty of cowardice.
>
> Catholic teaching sees these two distinct moral responses [legitimate defense and complete commitment to nonviolence] as having a complementary relationship, in the sense that both seek to serve the common good. They differ in their perception of how the common good is to be defended most effectively, but both responses testify to the Christian conviction that peace must be pursued and rights defended within moral restraints and in the context of defining other basic human values. (73–74)

Christians who commit themselves to nonviolent resistance are not passively accepting the presence of evil. Most are actively engaged in the peacemaking strategies already mentioned. Many are engaged in public witnesses for peace in society. Some even commit to international peacemaking through organizations like Christian Peacemaking Teams (see the sidebar "Christian Peacemaking Teams").

Not everyone is called to this commitment to nonviolent love. But those who are called to do so are powerful witnesses to the love of Jesus Christ. Their witness calls society to examine its attitude toward violence. Their witness is a reminder that true peace is achieved not through retaliation but through love. ✝

© David H. Wells/CORBIS

The people of the Philippines embraced nonviolence when challenging a fraudulent and immoral election. Through their efforts, many soldiers sent to attack them converted to their cause.

Live It!

Examples of Nonviolent Resistance

Many examples throughout history show how nonviolent resistance has brought about justice and peace in violent situations. You may wish to research the following historical situations and let them inspire you with the power of nonviolent love.

- In the 1920s and 1930s, Mahatma Gandhi organized and trained thousands of Indian citizens to nonviolently resist unjust laws under British colonial rule. Their efforts were a major factor leading to India's independence in 1947.
- In 1986 the people of the Philippines confronted the soldiers of President Ferdinand Marcos after the Church declared his presidential election fraudulent and immoral. When the soldiers attacked the protesters, the protesters knelt and prayed, refusing to give way. Many soldiers were converted to their cause. Marcos and his supporters were soon forced to leave the country.
- In the early 1980s, Polish workers organized a union called Solidarity to advocate for human rights and greater freedom. Inspired by the teachings of Pope Saint John Paul II, the group refused to use violence, even when many of the union's leaders were jailed or killed. Due to their efforts, Poland held its first free elections in 1989, and leaders from Solidarity won the elections.

Part Review

1. How is *violence* defined in Catholic social teaching?

2. Apply the spiral of violence to a real or imaginary conflict between nations. Describe the initial injustice and how it escalates at each stage of the spiral.

3. Why is war one of the greatest threats to the sacredness of human life?

4. Explain the conditions under which participating in war is morally justified.

5. Give two reasons why Catholic social teaching condemns the arms race.

6. Why do states have the moral responsibility to regulate the arms trade?

7. What three principles are important to keep in mind in responding to Christ's call to be peacemakers?

8. Describe at least four peacemaking strategies suggested by Catholic social teaching.

9. How would you respond to someone who says that loving your enemies is a sign of weakness?

Part 3

Protecting Dignity in Diversity

Reason and Revelation teach us a fundamental truth: all human beings are made in God's image and likeness. Every human being has a sacred dignity regardless of age, gender, color, race, physical appearance, or physical ability. But let's be clear about our diversity. We reflect God's image, not despite our being male or female but through our maleness or femaleness. We reflect God's likeness, not despite being black, brown, red, white, or yellow but through our ethnicity. God loves everyone, and he calls us to love and respect those who are different from us.

Unfortunately, human beings often find this hard to do. We are suspicious and even fearful of our physical and cultural differences—another unfortunate consequence of Original Sin. Our suspicion and fear become justification for ignoring, blaming, attacking, or using human beings who are different from us. At its worst this lack of respect for human dignity leads to the terrible evils of rape, slavery, segregation, war, and even genocide. We also see it expressed in prejudice, prostitution, pornography, economic exploitation, sexism, racism, and people's distrust of immigrants. These behaviors and attitudes are social sins because they have a negative impact on others and because they are encouraged by sinful social structures. Many social issues rooted in the lack of respect for human dignity have been addressed in Catholic social teaching.

The articles in this part address the following topics:

Article 36 Sexual Exploitation

There is no more fundamental difference among human beings than our sexuality, the gift of being female or male. God created the two sexes to be equal in dignity yet unique in some of their physical, emotional, and even spiritual characteristics. These differences make women and men complementary creatures, uniquely suited to loving each other intimately and raising a family together: "That is why a man leaves his father and mother and clings to his wife, and the two of them become one body" (Genesis 2:24). Women and men are called to acknowledge the dignity of their own sexual identity and accept the responsibility to live their sexual identity with integrity, according to the will of God.

When it is used immorally, sexuality also has great power to harm people and relationships. Two commandments forbid its misuse: the Sixth Commandment, "You shall not commit adultery," and the Ninth Commandment, "You shall not covet your neighbor's wife." These commandments remind us that sexual sin has social consequences. Not only do we harm our own integrity, but we can bring pain and suffering into the lives of many other people when we exploit others for our own sexual desires.

Human Sexuality: A Brief Overview

God created the two sexes as the foundation for human community. Our physical differences make it clear that men and women need each other in order to procreate. But our need to be in relationship with others is not for procreation only; it is God's plan that we live in relationship with others in order to also give love and receive love. Our human relationships should be an image of the loving communion of the Father, Son, and Holy Spirit, the primary communion that our human relationships share in. A person's sexuality is a part of every relationship he or she has, and finds

How does marriage fulfill God's plan for men and women to live in relationship?
© istock/rest

chastity

The virtue by which people are able to successfully and healthfully integrate their sexuality into their total person; recognized as one of the fruits of the Holy Spirit. Also one of the vows of religious life.

masturbation

Self-manipulation of one's sexual organs for the purpose of erotic pleasure or to achieve orgasm. It is a sin against the Sixth Commandment because the act cannot result in the creation of new life and because God created sexuality not for self-gratification but to unify a husband and wife in marriage.

fornication

Sexual intercourse between a man and a woman who are not married. It is morally wrong to engage in intercourse before marriage, a sin against the Sixth Commandment.

lust

Intense and uncontrolled desire for sexual pleasure. It is one of the seven capital sins.

its most complete fulfillment in marriage or in the practice of celibacy lived out in the priesthood.

The virtue of **chastity** helps us to live out our sexuality with integrity. Being a person of integrity means that nothing divides you; your inner life and your outer life are united. Thus a chaste person's thoughts, words, and actions all reflect God's purpose for the gift of sexuality. For example, a chaste person will not dress or act in ways to provoke the sexual passion of others, because the sexual act is for only a wife and husband to share. All people, married and unmarried, must practice chastity, using Jesus as the model for a chaste life. **Masturbation, fornication, pornography, lust,** and homosexual activity are among the sins that are serious offenses against the virtue of chastity.

Our sexuality, however, is not just an image of the divine communion of the Holy Trinity; it is also a call to share in God's life-giving power. This finds its full expression in the Sacrament of Matrimony. Marriage is a lifelong covenant of faithful love that a baptized man and a baptized woman freely enter into. In marriage a man and a woman promise to love each other completely and without conditions. In marriage a man and woman participate in God's life-giving power by bringing children into the world. For these reasons they must stay faithful to each other—emotionally, physically, and spiritually—throughout their entire life. **Adultery**, divorce, **polygamy**, and living together outside of marriage are serious offenses against the virtue of chastity and the Sixth Commandment and violate the dignity of marriage. These sins are a betrayal of the complete, lifelong commitment between one man and one woman that marriage requires. Strong and spiritually healthy marriages and families are the foundation of a healthy and just society. Any sin against the dignity of marriage and family also affects the common good of society.

Societal Exploitation of Sexuality

We now turn our attention to some sinful social structures that exploit human sexuality: prostitution, the pornography industry, sexual slavery, and the use of sex for marketing.

Sexism

A sexist person is someone who discriminates against people because of their gender. When this becomes a prevalent attitude in a society, then that society has developed the sinful social structure of **sexism.** Sexism takes many forms, including not allowing one gender equal rights in society (such as the right to vote); overlooking verbal, sexual, and physical abuse against one gender; and not allowing one gender equal work opportunities or equal pay for equal work. Across histories and cultures, sexism has most frequently been an offense against women.

The United States has undergone great social transformation in addressing sexism in the last one hundred years. In 1920 the nineteenth amendment to the Constitution gave women the right to vote in all state and federal elections. In 1963 the Equal Pay Act was passed to guarantee that men and women were paid the same wages for doing the same work. In 1972 Congress passed Title IX, a law requiring gender equity for boys and girls in every program receiving federal funding. (For example, prior to this law, most schools' sports programs were for boys only.) These changes in society have greatly reduced sexism in the United States, but they have not eliminated it. In 2009 women still earned only 77 percent of the average salaries that men earned (Institute for Women's Policy Research). Women typically have to put in more years of work before receiving promotions. They are ten times more likely to be the victims of abuse than men. Like all issues of social justice, we must be persistent in our efforts to transform the sinful social structures that perpetuate sexism.

Prostitution

Prostitution is the act of providing sexual services in exchange for money or some other form of payment. Prostitution is illegal in most U.S. states and in many countries around the world, but this has not eliminated it. According to the Black Market online database, prostitution generates more than $100 billion annually in revenue worldwide. Not only does prostitution encourage fornication and adultery but female and male prostitutes are often abused, demeaned, manipulated, and exposed to disease. Although those who earn income through prostitution often do so willingly, many women and children are forced into prostitution in a modern-day slave trade.

pornography
A written description or visual portrayal of a person or action that is created or viewed with the intention of stimulating sexual feelings. Creating or using pornography is a sin against the Sixth and Ninth Commandments.

© Andrew Holbrooke/Corbis

Sexuality is exploited and misused through sinful acts such as prostitution, sexual slave trade, and pornography. How is sexuality used to sell products in the mainstream media?

Sexual Slave Trade

The sexual slave trade, also called sex trafficking, involves forcing women, men, and children to work as prostitutes, perform in strip clubs, or make pornography. Sometimes these people are kidnapped and sold. Sometimes they are tricked; they are promised legitimate work, taken to another country, and then forced to work in the sex industry. The victims are often already vulnerable, such as runaway teens, people who are homeless, refugees, drug addicts, and women in poverty.

The Pornography Industry

The pornography industry creates and distributes sexually explicit stories, images, and video. The pornography industry in 2006 generated $97 billion worldwide and $13 billion in the U.S. alone ("Statistics on Pornography, Sexual Addiction and Online

Live It!

Avoiding Pornography

Pornography is a serious social sin. Unfortunately, many people fool themselves into believing that is not the case. "Who gets hurt?" they say. Or "I'm not really cheating on my spouse, because it is all fantasy." But consider these facts:

- Pornography is addictive. It directly affects the pleasure centers of the brain, much like using cocaine or other drugs. The younger a person is when he or she first uses pornography, the greater are his or her chances of becoming addicted.

- A high percentage of employees are use pornography during work hours, costing businesses millions of dollars in lost time every year. One in three businesses has fired an employee for using pornography.

- According to testimony presented before the U.S. Senate subcommittee in 2005, pornography negatively affects millions of marriages. Sixty-two percent of divorce lawyers surveyed said Internet pornography is a contributing factor in a significant number of divorce cases.

Considering these facts, the best and only safe way to deal with pornography is to avoid it completely. It is a great danger to your spiritual life, and using it will only encourage you to think of other people as objects for your gratification.

Racism is a sin, a sin that divides the human family, blots out the image of God among specific members of that family, and violates the fundamental human dignity of those called to be children of the same Father. Racism is the sin that says some human beings are inherently superior and others essentially inferior because of races. It is the sin that makes racial characteristics the determining factor for the exercise of human rights. It mocks the words of Jesus: "Treat others the way you would have them treat you."[4] Indeed, racism is more than a disregard for the words of Jesus; it is a denial of the truth of the dignity of each human being revealed by the mystery of the Incarnation.

Persons with Disabilities

People with physical, mental, emotional, or developmental disabilities are also the victims of prejudice and discrimination. We should remember that Jesus showed great concern for people with disabilities. When the disciples of John the Baptist asked him if he was the Messiah, Jesus answered, "Go and tell John what you hear and see: the blind regain their sight, the lame walk, lepers are cleansed, the deaf hear, the dead are raised, and the poor have the good news proclaimed to them" (Matthew 11:4–5).

As the Body of Christ, the Church is committed to ending discrimination against persons with disabilities, both within the Church and in society:

> The Church, through the response of her members to the needs of their neighbors and through its parishes, healthcare institutions and social service agencies, has always attempted to show a pastoral concern for individuals with disabilities. However, in a spirit of humble candor, we must acknowledge that at times we have responded to the needs of some of our people with disabilities only after circumstances or public opinion have compelled us to do so. By every means possible, therefore, the Church must continue to expand her healing ministry to these persons, helping them when necessary, working with them and raising her voice with them and with all members of society who are their advocates. ("Pastoral Statement of U.S. Catholic Bishops on Persons with Disabilities," 6)

Scripture and Tradition reveal that all people are one in Jesus Christ. God's plan of salvation restores the unity of the human race that was lost symbolically at the Tower of Babel (see Genesis 11:1–9). "From the day of Pentecost, when the Resurrection is announced to diverse peoples, each of whom understand it in their own language (cf. Acts of the Apostles 2:6), the Church fulfills her mission or restoring and bearing witness to the unity lost at Babel" (*Compendium of the Social Doctrine of the Church*, 431). This is why all Christians must remove racist stereotypes and prejudices from their hearts and minds. We must refuse to participate in racial discrimination of any kind. ✝

© Matt Cashore/University of Notre Dame

The hierarchy of the Church reflects the racial and ethnic diversity of God's children.

immigration, immigrant
The movement of a person or a group of people to a new country, usually to take up permanent residence. The opposite of immigration is emigration, the movement of people out of a country. An immigrant is a person who has moved to take up residence in another country.

migration, migrant
The movement of a person or a group of people from one place to another. A migrant moves from one place to another without establishing a permanent residence.

Article 38 Migration and Immigration

Immigration is a sensitive issue in our time, both politically and emotionally. Many Americans are concerned that native-born citizens have lost jobs to immigrants and that undocumented immigrants are costing taxpayers money. Other Americans believe that immigrants provide needed labor, doing jobs that native-born people don't want to do. Still others point out that the United States has always welcomed immigrants and refugees. Because of these and other conflicting concerns, emotions run high in debates and discussions about immigration, making it difficult to have a discussion based on reason and the values of the Gospel.

In the midst of this turmoil, the Church has been a voice of reason and moral clarity. The U. S. bishops have issued a series of statements addressing **migration** and immigration concerns since the 1990s: "From Newcomer to Citizens: All Come Bearing Gifts" (1999), "Welcoming the Stranger Among Us: Unity in Diversity" (2000), "Asian and Pacific Presence: Harmony in Faith" (2001), and "Strangers No

Longer: Together on the Journey of Hope" (cowritten with the bishops of Mexico, 2003). This article contains highlights from their teaching.

Keep in mind that it is often difficult to determine whether a person is a migrant or an immigrant. Sometimes people move to another country, usually because of war or poverty, without intending to settle there permanently. We would technically call these people refugees or migrants. Sometimes the situation in their homeland changes, and they can return. But often there is no change, and they remain in their new country for many years or even the rest of their lives. Are they then migrants or immigrants? The terms are often used interchangeably because of these circumstances.

Catholic Social Teaching on Migration and Immigration

Migration and immigration have been an integral part of salvation history. In the Old Testament, God called Abraham and Sarah to leave their homeland and immigrate to the land he led them to (see Genesis 12:1). In turn, they offered gracious hospitality to strangers traveling through their land

Pray It!

A Prayer for Migrants and Immigrants

Jesus,
Bless and protect those people forced to leave their homes,
especially because of war, persecution, poverty, and joblessness.
Keep safe their journeys to find a new home.
Help them to find places to live where they can build a new life
for themselves and their families.

Jesus, fill us with your compassion for the immigrants
who have settled in our cities, states, and country.
Give our leaders the wisdom to create legal and humane ways
to include those who hope to start a new life here.
Most of all, help us to see them as brothers and sisters
who need our love and support.
Amen.

diaspora

The movement, migration, or scattering of a people away from an established or ancestral homeland.

(see 18:1–8). Later Jacob and his children migrated to Egypt to survive a drought (see 47:1–6). Compassion for immigrants is enshrined in God's Covenant with the Israelites: "For the LORD, your God, . . . who executes justice for the orphan and the widow, and befriends the alien [foreigner], feeding and clothing him.So you too must befriend the alien, for you were once aliens yourselves in the land of Egypt" (Deuteronomy 10:17–19). Many Israelites became refugees and migrants during the Jewish **diaspora** following the destruction of the kingdoms of Israel (722 BC) and Judah (587 BC).

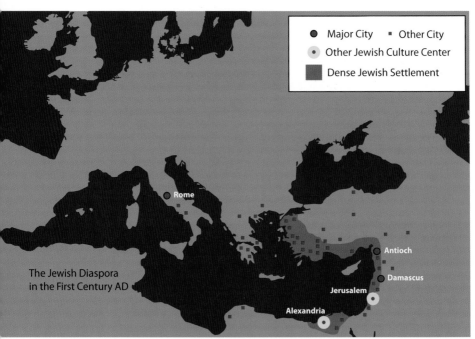

Major City ●   Other City ■

Other Jewish Culture Center ◉

Dense Jewish Settlement ▪

Rome

Antioch

Damascus

The Jewish Diaspora in the First Century AD

Jerusalem

Alexandria

© shutterstock/Mark Beckwith

In the New Testament, the Gospel of Matthew tells us that Jesus, Mary, and Joseph migrated to Egypt to escape King Herod's massacre of infant boys (see Matthew 2:13–15). They stayed there as refugees until Herod's death. "From this account the Holy Family has become a figure with whom Christian migrants and refugees throughout the ages can identify, giving them hope and courage in hard times" ("Strangers No Longer," 26). Jesus' Parable of the Last Judgment (see Matthew 25:31–46), in which he tells us to welcome the stranger, also speaks indirectly to caring for migrants and refugees. His commandment to "make disciples of all nations" and the missionary activity of the early Church make it clear that God's plan of salvation will unite people of all races into the one family of God.

Catholic social teaching builds on these biblical examples and principles. Beginning with *On the Condition of Labor (Rerum Novarum)* in 1891, the Church has recognized that migration and immigration are basic human rights, especially when injustice and violence make it difficult or even impossible for families and individuals to procure their basic rights. On the other hand, to minimize the need for people to leave their homes, the Church also calls for the elimination of the root causes of such migration: poverty, injustice, lack of religious freedom, and war. Pope Saint

Illegal Immigrants

The U.S. bishops have made a number of recommendations to provide a moral response to the issue of illegal aliens in the United States. Here are brief explanations of some of their main recommendations; however, it is best to read the bishops' complete letters and statements to fully understand their moral reasoning.

- Immigration laws should be reformed to make it possible for families to live together. Laws should not make spouses, parents, or children wait for years to join their loved ones who are legal residents.

- The U.S. government should provide a program to legalize undocumented immigrants who have lived and worked in the United States for many years. These undocumented workers already pay taxes and make an important contribution to society. Helping them to become legal citizens will ease many law enforcement problems and tensions.

- The U.S. government should provide greater opportunity for immigrants to legally enter the country in order to work. The U.S. economy depends on immigrants who work in jobs that are difficult to fill with native-born citizens. By issuing more work visas, the United States would diminish illegal border crossings and reduce the use of corrupt smugglers.

- The dignity and rights of immigrants who are caught trying to enter the United States illegally must be protected. Border enforcement should not push them to cross at locations where their lives are endangered. Migrants who are caught must be treated humanely, and their legal rights must be respected. Special care must be given to minors who are caught crossing alone, because of their vulnerability.

refugee
Any person who seeks protection in another country because of war or natural disaster or because of a well-founded fear of persecution in his or her native land.

Immigration is a sensitive issue in our time. How would you explain the Church teaching on immigration to a group discussing U.S. immigration policy?

John Paul II notes that ultimately the elimination of global poverty and injustice is the solution to the problem of illegal immigration (see "Message for World Migration Day," July 25, 1995).

Social Justice Principles on Migration and Immigration

The U.S. and Mexican bishops, in their letter "Strangers No Longer," identified the following five social justice principles that guide the Catholic perspective on migration and immigration issues:

I. **People have the right to find opportunities in their homeland.** The first principle is that no person should be forced to move from his or her home. The most common reasons that people are pressured to emigrate is the lack of jobs to support a family, the lack of basic necessities like food or clean water, and persecution because of religion, politics, or race. If every nation were to provide these basic needs and protect its people's human rights, then illegal immigration would dramatically decline.

II. **People have the right to migrate to support themselves and their families.** Recalling the principle that all the goods of the earth belong to all the people of the earth, the Church recognizes that when people cannot meet their basic needs or are being oppressed, they have a right to move somewhere else in order to survive and build a dignified life. All nations should respect this right and make provisions for legal immigration in these cases.

III. **Sovereign nations have the right to control their borders.** The right to migrate is not an absolute right. For example, nations have a right to exclude migrants who are not moving to escape starvation or oppression or criminal prosecution. On the other hand, justice requires that wealthier nations welcome immigrants who are escaping desperate situations.

© Karen Kasmauski/Science Faction/Corbis

IV. **Refugees and asylum seekers should be afforded protection.** Compassion calls for nations to protect **refugees** who are fleeing wars and persecution. These people should be provided a safe place to reside until the threat to their safety no longer exists.

V. **The human dignity and human rights of undocumented migrants and immigrants should be respected.** The Church never tires in reminding society that every person, no matter her or his legal or moral situation, has a sacred dignity that must be respected. This is of course true for undocumented migrants (also called illegal aliens) as well. The bishops remind us that undocumented migrants are typically pursuing the noble goal of building a life of dignity for themselves and their families. Governments must protect these undocumented migrants from abusive treatment and not pass laws meant primarily to punish them. ✝

Part Review

1. What does the virtue of chastity help us to do?

2. Describe three sinful social structures that support the exploitation of human sexuality.

3. What is racism?

4. Describe how stereotypes, negative prejudice, and discrimination contribute to racism.

5. Describe how migration and immigration have been a part of salvation history.

6. What are the five principles that guide the Catholic perspective on migration and immigration issues?

The Just Distribution of Material Goods

Part 1

Economic Justice

The principle of the universal destination of goods, that is, the principle that the earth's goods should be distributed fairly among all the people of the earth, has been mentioned several times in previous articles. It is one of the foundational principles of Catholic social teaching. The articles in this part apply that principle to some economic issues. The first article considers the related concerns of poverty and hunger. Though it is impossible to totally eliminate poverty here on earth, the widespread presence of poverty and hunger in the world are most often the result of sinful choices supported by sinful social structures. With the help of grace, we can identify the structures that contribute to this and work to change them.

The second article considers the important contribution that human work, also called labor, makes in the creation and distribution of the earth's resources. Through our work we participate in God's work of perfecting creation. Every person who can work has a duty to do so. But workers must also be treated justly so that the fruits of their labor allow them to create a life of dignity for themselves and their families.

The issues of poverty and work inevitably lead to questions about economic systems. Catholic social teaching provides important guidance on the moral dimensions of economics, including the strengths and weaknesses of different economic systems. A brief overview of these principles is presented in the third article.

The articles in this part address the following topics:

- Article 39: Hunger and Poverty (page 194)

- Article 40: Labor (page 201)

- Article 41: Economic Systems (page 206)

Article 39 Hunger and Poverty

colonialism

A policy by which a nation maintains or exerts its control over a foreign territory or country.

The United Nations Food and Agricultural Organization estimated that 925 million people suffered from hunger in 2010. That's about one seventh of the world's population. They also estimated that in 2005 about 1.4 billion people lived in extreme poverty, which is defined as less than $1.25 a day (by contrast, the average U.S. citizen lives on about $100 a day). That's one fifth of the world's population. The good news is that the worldwide poverty rate has steadily fallen during the last three decades. But the number of hungry and desperately poor people in the world remains staggering.

Poverty and hunger exist in the United States too, and the rate has been increasing in recent years. According to the organization Bread for the World, approximately one in eight U.S. citizens lived below the poverty line in 2009 (which is $21,756 for a family of four). Children are particularly at risk; one in five lives below the poverty line and one in four is at risk for hunger. The statistics are worse for African-American and Latino children: one in three is at risk of hunger. These statistics raise an important social justice question. If God created the world to provide what every human being needs to thrive, then why are so many people struggling just to survive?

Fighting Poverty and Hunger

People are not poor and hungry because God made a mistake. The natural disasters that are part of the fallen state of the world cause only a small fraction of the world's poverty and hunger. Poverty and hunger result primarily from human sin that is supported by sinful social structures. The earth provides enough resources for every human being to live with dignity. In fact, there is enough food grown in the world for every man, woman, and child to consume 3,600 calories per day, which is far more than the average person needs. The United Nations Development Program has estimated that the basic nutrition and health needs of the world's poorest people could be met by spending only an additional $13 billion a year (Bread for the World). That's less money than the people of the United States and the European Union spend on pet food.

Percentage of People Living in Extreme Poverty by Region of the World

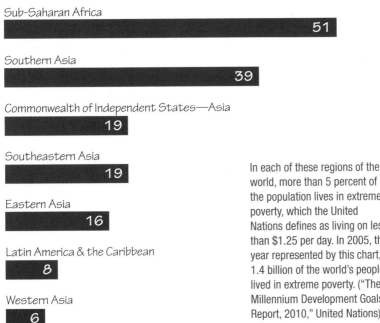

Sub-Saharan Africa
51

Southern Asia
39

Commonwealth of Independent States—Asia
19

Southeastern Asia
19

Eastern Asia
16

Latin America & the Caribbean
8

Western Asia
6

In each of these regions of the world, more than 5 percent of the population lives in extreme poverty, which the United Nations defines as living on less than $1.25 per day. In 2005, the year represented by this chart, 1.4 billion of the world's people lived in extreme poverty. ("The Millennium Development Goals Report, 2010," United Nations)

Widespread poverty and hunger are not inevitable. The sinful structures that support hunger and poverty can be changed, especially through the conversion of people's hearts so that we have a greater compassion for those who are suffering. Here are some brief descriptions of some of the structures that need to be addressed.

Lack of Democratic Governments

Many of the countries with widespread poverty and hunger are ruled by a tiny group of people who came to power and remain in power through violence and corruption. In many cases these elite rulers are a legacy of **colonialism**. Between 1500 and 1900, European countries invaded and conquered many native peoples around the globe, making them colonies of European nations. By 1914, Europe, its colonies, and its

democracy
A governmental system in which the political power is held by the people of the state, who freely elect their leaders.

infrastructure
The basic facilities, services, and physical systems needed for the functioning of a community or society. Examples include public education, transportation, water supply, and energy supply systems.

former colonies (including the United States) controlled 84 percent of the world's people. In many cases a small group of people were put in power in each colony to ensure that goods and taxes were sent back to the ruling nations in Europe. In the second half of the twentieth century, many of those colonized nations gained their independence. However, even after the European colonial powers relinquished their authority over the former colonies, the pattern of an elite group governing the country had been established and was often continued by powerful native people.

Elite rulers who come to power by privilege or force or corruption rarely rule with the common good in mind. They do not develop laws and economic policies that raise people out of poverty; rather, their policies protect and increase their own wealth and power. For example, they raise crops to sell for personal profit—such as coffee, tea, and sugar—instead of using the land to grow beans, corn, and rice to feed the local population. If foreign aid is sent to help reduce poverty or hunger, these elite rulers find ways to divert the money for their personal wealth. Even in advanced democracies like the United States, small groups of powerful people can have greater political influence than their numbers alone would suggest.

Every society's practices and moral choices reflect that society's vision of human purpose and human destiny. Unless this vision is informed by God's revealed truth, this vision is misinformed. This is why many societies throughout history have not placed a high value on freedom, thus becoming totalitarian states in which one person or a small group makes decisions affecting the rest of society. For this reason Catholic social teaching endorses **democracy** as one part of the solution to poverty and hunger. Pope Saint John Paul II clearly expresses this in his social encyclical *Hundredth Year (Centesimus Annus)*.

> The Church values the democratic system inasmuch as it ensures the participation of citizens in making political choices, guarantees to the governed the possibility both of electing and holding accountable those who govern them, and of replacing them through peaceful means when appropriate. Thus she cannot encourage the formation of narrow ruling groups which usurp the power of the State for individual interests or for ideological ends. (46)

The Catholic Church Is Fighting Poverty

The Catholic Church has participated in the fight against poverty from its beginnings. Here are just a few contemporary examples:

- Almost every diocese in the United States has a Catholic Charities agency that serves the poor and vulnerable within its diocese.
- Saint Vincent de Paul societies serve those in need through secondhand stores, food pantries, and emergency funds.
- Many religious communities, such as the Sisters of the Poor, the Daughters of Charity, and the Missionaries of Charity, are specifically dedicated to serving the poor.

At the national level, the Catholic Church in the United States has two organizations dedicated to fighting hunger and poverty. The Catholic Campaign for Human Development (CCHD) focuses its efforts on poverty within the United States. The CCHD's mission is to "address the root causes of poverty in America through promotion and support of community-controlled, self-help organizations and through transformative education" (from the CCHD Web site).

Catholic Relief Services (CRS) is one of the largest non-governmental international aid organizations in the United States. Most people are familiar with its Lenten poverty awareness and donation program called Operation Rice Bowl. CRS's mission is to carry out the "commitment of the Bishops of the United States to assist the poor and vulnerable overseas" (from the CRS Web site). CRS has helped the poorest of the poor in over a hundred countries around the world.

A Lack of Development

Another primary cause of poverty is the lack of the **infrastructures** that people need in order to build a life with dignity. For example, in a country lacking a strong system of public education, the majority of people will be illiterate and will lack the education they need to determine their own destiny. In a village that lacks an infrastructure for water supply—a way to deliver clean drinking water—women and children will be forced to spend hours every day transporting water from a river or spring miles away—hours that

development
To help provide the social structures that are necessary so a person or group of people can build a life of dignity and respond to their vocation according to God's call.

Through programs that help families and individuals, organizations such as Catholic Relief Services and Caritas International work for economic and social development. Individuals can contribute to their good works through the donation of time and resources.

could be used for education or for running a home business. The lack of clean water also leads to the spread of diseases. Helping people in these situations means building the infrastructures they need, such as a free public education system or a system of village wells, to give them the opportunity to create secure and dignified lives, with the ability to rise out of poverty.

Creating the necessary infrastructures so that a people can build a life of dignity is called **development.** Keep in mind that true development is more than just economic development, such as helping people to grow more food or to make more money. It concerns the development of the whole person, so it means helping people to grow personally and spiritually, enabling them to respond to their vocation and therefore to God's call.

Catholic social teaching strongly advocates development as a goal that will help to alleviate poverty and hunger. This means providing the infrastructures for education, fair trade, health care, better transportation systems, and so on. It is a work of justice because it helps people to live more dignified lives. When pope, Saint John Paul II called for it to become a worldwide effort:

> This is the culture which is hoped for, one which fosters trust in the human potential of the poor, and consequently in their ability to improve their condition through work or to make a positive contribution to economic prosperity. . . . [This] calls for a *concerted worldwide effort to promote development,* an effort which also involves sacrificing the positions of income and of power enjoyed by the more developed economies. (*Hundredth Year,* 52)

© Lane Hartill/Catholic Relief Services

There are many organizations dedicated to this work, such as the Catholic Campaign for Human Development, Catholic Relief Services, Caritas International, The Water Project, Heifer International, religious communities like Maryknoll, and many others.

The Gap between Rich and Poor

There is a large gap in wealth between the world's richest and poorest citizens. The 2010 United States census revealed that the top 20 percent of U.S. wage earners received 50 percent of the nation's total income, while the bottom 20 percent of wage earners received only 3.4 percent of the total income (Huffington Post). A World Institute for Development Economics' study reveals that this situation is even worse worldwide; the richest 1 percent of the world's adults owns 40 percent of the world's assets, while half the world's population owns only 1 percent of the world's assets.

The primary cause for this inequity is greed and the lack of social structures to prevent this unequal distribution of the earth's goods. This structure is perpetuated because wealthy people have the resources to influence economic systems and governments in ways that favor them and enable them to maintain their wealth. In their pastoral letter *Economic Justice for All*, the U.S. bishops give voice to the urgency of addressing these unjust and sinful social structures:

> Unequal distribution [of income and wealth] should be evaluated in terms of several moral principles we have enunciated: the priority of meeting the basic needs of the poor and the importance of increasing the level of participation by all members of society in the economic life of the nation. These norms establish a strong presumption against extreme inequality of income and wealth as long as there are poor, hungry, and homeless people in our midst. They also suggest that extreme inequalities are detrimental to the development of social solidarity and community. In view of these norms we find the disparities of income and wealth in the United States to be unacceptable. Justice requires that all members of our society work for economic, political and social reforms that will decrease these inequities. (185)

Catholic social teaching does not teach that everyone should receive the same wages. In fact, it teaches that some

just wage

A salary that recognizes the value of the work being performed and that is high enough to allow the laborer and his or her immediate family to live a life of human dignity. Minimally, this means a wage above the poverty line.

inequality is good because it provides incentives for owners and workers to work harder and smarter and to take greater risks, which can benefit the common good. But the equal dignity of human persons requires that we work to reduce excessive social and economic inequities.

Lack of Jobs That Pay Just Wages

It only stands to reason that if all people had work that paid a **just wage,** poverty would be greatly reduced. *Economic Justice for All* states the following:

> *The first line of attack against poverty must be to build and sustain a healthy economy that provides employment opportunities at just wages for all adults who are able to work.* Poverty is intimately linked to the issue of employment. Millions are poor because they have lost their jobs or because their wages are too low. . . . Expanded employment especially in the private sector would promote human dignity, increase social solidarity, and promote self reliance of the poor. (196)

This is a case, however, in which the most obvious solution is the most difficult to achieve. There are many complex reasons behind unemployment and poor wages. If we start working on this issue, we will quickly be led to

Live It!

What You Can Do

You can make a difference in the fight against poverty and hunger. Here are a few suggestions:

- Live a simpler lifestyle. Buy fewer things new and buy more things used. Trade books, games, movies, and clothes with friends. Use fewer disposable products. Donate money you save to Church agencies that finance development projects in impoverished areas of the world.
- Support your local economy and local workers. Encourage your family to buy more locally grown food and locally made products.
- Volunteer to help at a food pantry, soup kitchen, or some other food distribution program in your community.
- Work for more affordable housing in your community by getting involved with charitable housing organizations such as Habitat for Humanity.
- Support the advocacy efforts of the United States Conference of Catholic Bishops or of your diocese to reduce poverty at home and abroad.

other issues, including the ones already mentioned: the lack of democratic processes, the need for development, and the gap between the rich and the poor. But the bottom line is that the Seventh Commandment, "You shall not steal," calls employers to practice love and justice in distributing wealth and in compensating people for their work. The first social encyclical of the modern era, *On the Condition of Labor* (*Rerum Novarum*), emphasizes this point:

labor
Human work.

> [The employer's] great and principal duty is to give everyone what is just. Doubtless, before deciding whether wages are fair, many things have to be considered; but wealthy owners and all masters of labor should be mindful of this—that to exercise pressure upon the indigent and the destitute for the sake of gain, and to gather one's profit out of the need of another, is condemned by all laws, human and divine. (20) ☦

Article 40 Labor

The question of human work, also called **labor** in Catholic social teaching, is directly tied to the question of the just distribution of the world's resources. Through our labor we make use of the world's resources and distribute them among the world's people. This is part of God's plan of Creation. The second Creation account teaches this truth with these words: "The LORD God then took the man and settled him in the garden of Eden, to cultivate and care for it" (Genesis 2:15). In other words, God put Adam to work, in order to produce the things Adam and his family would need to live with dignity. Notice that Adam would do it respectfully, caring for the earth at the same time he was cultivating it.

Catholic social teaching has a lot to say about human work. One whole chapter in the *Compendium of the Social Doctrine of the Church* is devoted to this topic. This article summarizes important points in three areas: the purpose of work, the duty to work, and workers' rights.

The Purpose of Work

As already mentioned, human work is a part of God's plan of Creation. Through our labor we participate in his work of

capital

The material, financial, and human resources needed to start and run a business.

creation. God calls us to be his partners by using and caring for the earth's resources for the benefit of all people and even of all creation. This calling is a noble privilege and a high honor. Some people might say, "Work is not an honor, it is a boring and difficult necessity." It is true that work is sometimes tedious and unpleasant. But this was not God's original plan for human work; this is a consequence of Original Sin. The Book of Genesis states this consequence specifically:

> To the man he said: "Because you listened to your wife and ate
> from the tree of which I had forbidden you to eat,
> Cursed be the ground because of you!
>> In toil shall you eat its yield
>> all the days of your life.
> Thorns and thistles shall it bring forth to you,
>> as you eat of the plants of the field.
> By the sweat of your face
>> shall you get bread to eat."
>
> (3:17–19)

Labor and Capital

In economics, **capital** is a term used to describe several things: (1) the material things needed to create a product or provide a service, (2) the money needed to start a business, and (3) the human skills and knowledge necessary for a business to be successful. Labor and capital have a complementary relationship; a business needs both workers and equipment and finances in order to succeed. However, Catholic social teaching emphasizes that workers have priority over capital. To put it another way, a business's people are more important than its equipment and finances.

This means workers should never be put at personal risk in order to save or protect a piece of equipment or in order to save money. Similarly, the workforce should not be reduced primarily to increase profits. Making workers the priority over capital also requires that workers not be overworked by the amount of work they have to do or forced into making their job the only priority of their life. When employers and workplaces make workers their priority, the true meaning of work in God's plan of creation is achieved. Such businesses are often more successful because workers who are treated well have greater productivity.

The religious truth being conveyed is that before Original Sin, work was joyful because the earth easily provided what was necessary to live. But after the Fall, the relationship between human beings and the earth was damaged and so work became more difficult, requiring greater effort. But Christ's saving work has redeemed all of creation so we can labor knowing that our right relationship with the earth will also be restored in the New Creation (see Romans 8:19–21).

Jesus is a model for our work. He described his mission as work: "My Father is at work until now, so I am at work" (Matthew 5:17). We presume that in his early years he worked as a carpenter, taking up Joseph's trade. During his ministry he worked tirelessly, preaching, healing, and traveling to announce

© Scala/Ministero per i Beni e le Attività culturali / Art Resource, NY

the Kingdom of God. His work was for the salvation of the world. Our work too can share in his saving work if we unite our labor to his. This does not mean that we have to do the same work that Jesus did. It does mean that we should choose work that is moral and contributes to dignity of human beings and the common good. And it means that we should perform our work with gratitude, joy, and justice.

How has Original Sin altered God's plan for human work? How does looking to Jesus as our model affect what work we choose to do?

Duty to Work

Work is not an option; every person who is able to work has a duty to do so. We see this in the New Testament when Saint Paul says to the early Christians, "We instructed you that if anyone was unwilling to work, neither should that one eat" (2 Thessalonians 3:10). It seems that some members of the Christian community in the city of Thessalonica felt they would be supported by the community even if they didn't work. Paul makes it clear that this is an unacceptable attitude within the Christian community.

Work is a duty because the fruit of human labor results in the necessities of life for workers and their families. Whether a person's work results in the direct production of food or in earning a wage, work is the societal means required to create or to purchase food, clothing, and housing. But earning our own living is not the only reason God calls us to work. Another reason is because through work we contribute to the common good. Through work we participate in God's work of creating a more beautiful and just world. Work provides food, homes, clothing, education, energy, art, entertainment, and information. Works of charity help people who are poor and vulnerable to improve the quality of their lives. Working for justice changes social structures that perpetuate injustice and builds social structures that help to ensure human rights so that all people can live with greater dignity.

© shutterstock/Francesco Ridolfi

It is important to remember that there are many diverse kinds of work that all contribute to the common good. And there are many important kinds of work in which the worker is not paid a wage. The parent whose primary work is staying at home to raise and support the family's children is doing very important work. So are people who volunteer in charitable organizations. This is why Catholic social teaching insists that laborers are paid wages that can support a spouse and the family's children so that both parents do not have to work at paying jobs (see the *Compendium of the Social Doctrine of the Church*, 250).

We each have a duty to work, whether as a student, parent, employee, or volunteer. What type of attitude does God want us to have when we work?

Workers' Rights

Because of the centrality of labor in God's plan for creation, Catholic social teaching places a strong emphasis on the just treatment of workers. It describes the rights that workers should enjoy so that their dignity is respected and that the value of their work is properly recognized. The first and most important right is the right to work itself. Society should be structured so that every person is able to find meaningful work. Just as the earth provides enough goods so that every person should be able to live with dignity, so too there is enough work for every person to contribute to the common good in a meaningful way. In addition to this most basic right, here are some other rights identified in the *Compendium of the Social Doctrine of the Church;*

- Workers have a right to participate in the ownership, decision making, and profits of the businesses they work for. When workers are invested in this way, they will feel respected as persons and will be motivated to do their work well. (See 281)

- Workers have a right to rest from work. The Third Commandment, "Remember to keep holy the sabbath day" (Exodus 20:8) reminds us that workers should have time off from work to spend with their families, for prayer and worship, for community involvement, and for works of charity and justice. (See 284–286)

- Women have an important contribution to make in society, including the workplace. They should not be discriminated against in the workplace. They should receive equal pay and benefits. (See 295)

Pray It!

Prayer for Labor

The following prayer is adapted from the prayers in the Mass for the Blessing of Human Labor *(Roman Missal):*

> Oh God,
> who through human labor
> never cease to perfect and govern the vast work of creation,
> listen to the supplications of your people
> and grant that all men and women
> may find work that befits their dignity,
> joins them more closely to one another
> and enables them to serve their neighbor.
> Through the work you have given us to do
> may we sustain our life on earth
> and trustingly build up your Kingdom.
> We ask this through Christ our Lord.
> Amen.

strike

An organized work stoppage whereby workers refuse to work in order to gain public support and to pressure their employer to address their rights.

capitalism

An economic system based on the private ownership of goods and the free-market system.

socialism

An economic system in which there is no private ownership of goods and the creation and distribution of goods and services is determined by the whole community or by the government.

- Workers have a right to a just wage. A just wage is enough money to ensure that the worker can purchase the necessities needed so the worker and his or her immediate family do not need to live in poverty. (See 302–303)

- In order to advocate for their rights, workers have the right to form labor unions and associations, and to **strike** when it is necessary to protect their rights. Strikes should be used as a last resort and should always be peaceful. Labor unions help workers to defend their rights, but they need to work collaboratively with employers. (See 304–307) ✝

Article 41 Economic Systems

If a society is committed to ending poverty and hunger, to providing meaningful work for all its citizens, and to protecting worker's rights, an important question still remains. How should it structure its economic system in order to accomplish these goals? Capitalism and socialism are the two prominent economic systems used in the world today to reach these goals. You have probably heard discussion about the pros and cons of these systems. Politicians love to throw around the terms *capitalism* and *socialism,* often in ways meant to stereotype their opponents. But these concepts are too important to be treated simplistically. Catholic social teaching takes the issue of economic systems very seriously and offers deep insights into their moral strengths and weaknesses.

We must start with the truth that the human person is "the author, center, and goal of all economic and social life" (*Catechism of the Catholic Church,* 2459). God has revealed that the earthly goods he created are meant for all people, not just a privileged few. Thus a moral economic system must ensure that the just distribution of the earth's goods takes place. This can happen only when the people who participate in our economic systems are motivated not by greed but by love of neighbor and a commitment to the common good.

The Free Market

Human freedom is one of the most important gifts that human beings have received from God. Our freedom gives us the capacity to love God and others, or not to. It gives us the ability to make moral choices, and it is the basis for a moral and effective market system. Catholic social teaching endorses the **free market** because of its proven capacity to effectively deliver goods and services. A free market is a market system in which individuals and businesses are free to create and sell whatever goods and services they wish to sell at whatever price they wish to charge. Because in a free market businesses compete with one another for consumers' money, businesses strive to keep the cost of producing their products low and generally charge lower prices than they would if there were no competition.

free market
A market system in which individuals and businesses are free to create and sell whatever goods and services they wish to sell at whatever prices they wish to charge.

© Nick Gunderson/CORBIS

The Church endorses the free market as a morally effective way to produce and deliver goods and services. The primary purpose of business is not to make money; it is to contribute to the common good and the development of the human person.

The free market provides the means to accomplish many of the objectives required for justice. For example, a free market should do the following

- respond to people's needs for important products and services
- help to keep prices low and businesses' profit goals fair to consumers
- encourage individuals and businesses to be creative and to take risks in developing new and better products and services
- encourage businesses to be efficient and to practice conservation of the earth's resources

These benefits would not occur in tightly controlled or excessively regulated markets, such as those in Communist countries. Political authority must respect the moral order and must protect the legitimate exercise of human freedom. The freedom to create and run a business is a critical and legitimate use of human freedom.

But Catholic social teaching also is clear that the free market must have moral constraints. The most important moral consideration is that every business must contribute to the common good and to authentic human development. The primary purpose of a business is not just to make money. So, for example, selling illegal drugs, making and distributing pornography, and providing abortion services might be free-market enterprises, but they are immoral businesses because they hurt the common good and do not contribute to authentic human development.

Capitalism and Socialism

It follows that if the free market is necessary for a moral and effective economic system, then the best economic system is the one that is based on a free market. This is the fundamental reason why Catholic social teaching condemns socialism. Socialism, in its purest form, is an economic system that rejects private ownership of property in favor of communal ownership of all property, including all capital. It promises that no one will go wanting for the necessities of life. In

Catholic Wisdom

The State's Role in Economics

In Catholic social teaching, the state has an important responsibility in free-market economies.

It is necessary for the market and the State to act in concert, one with the other, and to complement each other mutually. In fact, the free market can have a beneficial influence on the general public only when the State is organized in such a manner that it defines and gives direction to economic development, promoting the observation of fair and transparent rules, and making direct interventions—only for the length of time strictly necessary[1]— when the market is not able to obtain the desired efficiency and when it is a question of putting the principle of redistribution into effect. (*Compendium of the Social Doctrine of the Church*, 353) theory this might seem good, because if everyone owned everything, then the goods of the earth would be fairly distributed to every person. In practice, however, this never works for long.

The socialist ideals taught by Karl Marx (1818–1883) and other thinkers of his time became the basis for modern Communism. But socialism never ended up fulfilling the promise of becoming a fair and just economic system. The power to control the distribution of wealth and the systems of production always ends in the hands of an elite group of powerful people. The majority of people are left without any power or way to participate in the decision-making process. The result is that "the sources of wealth themselves would run dry, for no one would have any interest in exerting his talents or his industry; and that ideal equality about which they entertain pleasant dreams would be in reality the leveling down of all to a like condition of misery and degradation" (*On the Condition of Labor*, 15). Over a hundred years ago, in the first social encyclical of the modern era, Pope Leo XIII reached the conclusion that "it is clear that the main tenet of socialism, community of goods, must be utterly rejected, since it only injures those whom it would seem meant to benefit, is directly contrary to the natural rights of mankind, and would introduce confusion and disorder into the [general population]" (*On the Condition of Labor*, 15).

© istock/Rubén Hidalgo

The socialist ideals of Karl Marx became the foundation for modern Communism. Why does the Church condemn socialism and Communism as economic and political systems?

This leaves capitalism as the other main economic system. Capitalism is based on the private ownership of property and the free-market system. Catholic social teaching endorses capitalism for these reasons but with some qualifications. Pope Saint John Paul II explains the reason for this qualified endorsement:

> The answer [to whether capitalism is good] is obviously complex. If by "capitalism" is meant an economic system which recognizes the fundamental and positive role of business, the market, private property and the resulting responsibility for the means of production, as well as free human creativity in the economic sector, then the answer is certainly in the

affirmative, even though it would perhaps be more appropriate to speak of a "business economy," "market economy" or simply "free economy." But if by "capitalism" is meant a system in which freedom in the economic sector is not circumscribed within a strong juridical framework [system of laws and regulations] which places it at the service of human freedom in its totality, and which sees it as a particular aspect of that freedom, the core of which is ethical and religious, then the reply is certainly negative. (*Hundredth Year*, 42)

The Pope is saying is that capitalism is the means to a greater good; it is not the good itself. Capitalism will lead to a just economic system only if the people in the system are motivated by a moral commitment to the common good. When the people in a capitalist system are motivated by greed, they will use the system to increase their own wealth at the expense of the other people's rights and dignity. And when this happens, it is often the poor and vulnerable who suffer the most. There are many examples of abuses in capitalist systems that lead to greater numbers of poor and vulnerable people.

True Success

The belief that people's success and happiness is determined by their wealth has existed in many different cultures throughout history. It is true that if a person does not have enough money to pay for adequate food and housing, then his or her life will be difficult. But once a person has enough wealth to provide for the basic necessities of a dignified life, increased wealth will not necessarily bring increased happiness. In fact, just the opposite may be true.

We have already seen in article 7, "Social Teaching in the New Testament," that Jesus Christ taught that people who are truly blessed have a detachment from wealth; they do not make the accumulation of money their life's goal. True and lasting fulfillment is found in becoming more like Christ and in following his plan for our lives. This is the fulfillment that leads to inner peace and joy. As we grow in our spiritual lives, we come to understand that the truly successful person is the one who is open to the infinite love of God and who accepts what God has revealed about the purpose of life.

So Catholic social teaching calls for the government and the business community to work together. At times, even in a capitalist system, the government has a responsibility to provide laws and regulations that guarantee that its citizens have the freedom to actively participate in the economic structures that affect them and that there is a fair distribution of the earth's goods. Laws protecting consumers' rights, setting minimum wages, protecting the environment, and limiting business monopolies would be examples of such laws and regulations. ✝

Part Review

1. Explain why widespread poverty and hunger are not inevitable.

2. Describe several social structures that contribute to poverty and hunger.

3. Why do human beings have a duty to work?

4. What four important workers' rights are identified in Catholic social teaching?

5. Why does Catholic social teaching endorse the free-market system?

6. Why is Catholic social teaching's endorsement of capitalism a qualified endorsement and not an unqualified endorsement?

Part 2

Care for the Earth

The Second Vatican Ecumenical Council reminded us that "God has destined the earth and everything it contains for all peoples and nations." The goods of creation belong to humanity as a whole. Yet the current pace of environmental exploitation is seriously endangering the supply of certain natural resources not only for the present generation, but for generations yet to come. It is not hard to see that environmental degradation is often due to the lack of far-sighted official policies or to the pursuit of myopic economic interests, which then, tragically, become a serious threat to creation. To combat this phenomenon, economic activity needs to consider that "every economic decision has a moral consequence" and thus show increased respect for the environment. ("Message of His Holiness Pope Benedict XVI for the Celebration of the World Day of Peace, January 1, 2010," 7)

The words of Pope Benedict XVI brilliantly summarize the reasons behind the growing ecological crises in the world. God created the world so all its creatures—including human beings—would be interdependent, connected in a harmonious web of life. He intended human beings to be caretakers and stewards of creation in order to protect and develop this harmony. Unfortunately, humanity has not practiced this stewardship faithfully, resulting in serious environmental damage and ecological crises that threaten to become worldwide disasters. We need to take seriously our call to be stewards and improve our relationship with the earth to prevent more serious damage, both for ourselves and for future generations.

The articles in this part address the following topics:

Keys to Stewardship

If we are to successfully answer God's call to be good stewards of creation, we need to learn from the lessons of the Genesis Creation accounts. Let's take a deeper look at how those lessons might guide our relationship with the natural world today.

Respect for the Sacramental Universe

"He found it very good" (Genesis 1:31). These words signal not only the dignity of human beings but also the basic goodness of all of creation, which flows from the goodness of God. So many people become keenly aware of the presence of God when they stop to ponder the beauty, complexity, power, and mystery of creation. This is why the U.S. bishops described the universe as sacramental: because it reveals the presence of God in a visible and tangible way (see *Renewing the Earth*, 6). Each bird, fish, and blade of grass is his work of art and therefore has value on its own, apart from its relationship to people.

God's presence in the natural world reminds us of our own place within the whole of creation: we are creation's caretakers, not its creator. Acknowledging this helps us to avoid acting like "gods" who have absolute power over creation: "Dwelling in the presence of God, we begin to experience ourselves *as part of creation*, as stewards *within it*, not separate from it" (*Renewing the Earth*, 6, emphasis added). Respect for creation, which is the foundation of stewardship, is based on respect for God's presence in it.

A Gift for the Common Good

"See, I have give you every seed-bearing plant . . . to be your food" (Genesis 1:29). God intends for humans to benefit from creation, creating a good life for themselves and others. People need the earth's natural resources, and have a right to use them. That is why God gives us dominion over the earth (see 1:28).

Unfortunately, these words have often been interpreted to mean that God gives humans ownership of the earth, in the sense of having absolute power over it. But the overall message of Catholic social teaching is that the land ultimately belongs to God, who intends that it be used for the common good: "God has given the fruit of the earth to sustain the entire human family 'without excluding or favoring anyone'" (*Renewing the Earth*, 7). Part of the responsibility of stewardship, then, involves safeguarding natural resources to ensure that they benefit *all* people, including poor people and future generations—not just those powerful enough to control them.

Caring for Creation

We are not gods over creation. But as images of God, we are called to reflect his care for creation. In the first Creation account, God provides not only for the well-being of the human community but also for all living creatures (see Genesis 1:29–30). Therefore the right to use natural resources for the good of humanity is balanced by the responsibility to ensure the well-being of the natural world.

At a minimum, caring for creation involves respecting its limits. In the Old Law, for instance, every seventh year was to be "a year of sabbath rest for the land" (Leviticus 25:5), during which it was not to be farmed. Part of the challenge of stewardship today is recognizing the earth's need for "rest" from human consumption. In *Renewing the Earth,* the U.S. Catholic bishops call for sustainable economic practices. Sustainable economic practices use natural resources in a way that preserves the earth's ability to nurture itself and the whole human community well into the future. Nonsustainable practices, on the other hand, focus on short-term benefits of using the earth's resources and lead to long-term harm of the earth and its inhabitants. ✝

© Mika/Corbis

Small acts, such as recycling or planting trees, can make a big difference for the long-term care of the environment.

Catholic Social Teaching Documents

Catholic social teaching has been a strong and consistent voice for the stewardship of creation in the last twenty-five years. The following documents are excellent resources that can easily be found online:

- "Message of His Holiness Pope John Paul II for the Celebration of the World Day of Peace, January 1, 1990" (the ecological crisis)
- *Renewing the Earth: An Invitation to Reflection and Action on Environment in Light of Catholic Social Teaching* (U.S. bishops' statement, 1991)
- *Global Climate Change: A Plea for Dialogue, Prudence, and the Common Good* (U.S. bishops' statement, 2001)
- "Message of his Holiness Pope Benedict XVI's for the Celebration of the World Day of Peace, January 1, 2010" (cultivate peace, protect creation)

Article 44 Stewardship, Not Exploitation

The current environmental crises make it increasingly urgent that we respond to the call to stewardship by respecting the integrity of creation. Unfortunately, all too often humanity is guilty of exploiting creation rather than caring for it as good stewards. Fulfilling our God-given role as true stewards of creation means practicing sustainable economics. This will happen only when we consider the long-term consequences of the decisions we make as individuals and as a society.

That is often easier said than done, but the good news is that many people are already learning to sustain the earth by tapping into their God-given creativity. This article provides some principles and examples for becoming better stewards.

Environmental Accounting

Consumption of natural resources is one of the leading causes of environmental damage, because often resources are consumed without considering the effects on the environment. One way people are beginning to respect the limits of creation is through **environmental accounting,** which seeks to include the value of the environment when making economic decisions.

What is the value of clean air or clean water? What is the value of a honeybee or a wetland? In a culture that measures worth primarily in financial terms, these natural resources have often been undervalued. If we place little value on the natural environment, we are likely to exploit it in order to gain something of greater short-term economic value. For example, if we cannot sell clean air and yield a profit, why should we worry about any air pollution a profitable factory might create?

© shutterstock/NatUlrich

Such short-term thinking fails to reflect the real value of the environment. In order to be good stewards of creation, we need to take into account the true value of the earth and its goods. When making business decisions, we must consider the following factors to do a true environmental accounting (also called "green accounting"):

- **The hidden economic value** Natural resources that might not appear to have much economic value actually make a huge indirect contribution to the economy. According to researchers, the environment's "free" services—from providing water and creating soil to treating waste and pollinating crops—contribute around $33 trillion annually to the global economy (Robert Costanza, et al., "The Value of the World's Ecosystem Services and Natural Capital," in *Nature*).

- **The value for life** Sometimes the value of natural resources is difficult to measure in economic terms, even though they are important to human life. For example, how do you measure the value of clean air or drinking water? Yet because of polluted air and water, many people are already spending money on air and water purifiers. Businesses and government organizations are spending millions of dollars cleaning up polluted rivers and lakes. These costs must be taken into account in order to do a true environmental accounting. Without change, the costs of repairing the damage human beings are causing to the natural resources that are crucial to our survival will only increase in the future.

- **The value as a gift from God** Natural resources have a God-given value that cannot be measured in terms of money. Good stewardship involves asking whether consuming a natural resource will benefit human life and dignity more than it will harm the environment in the long run. Taking the value of the environment into account can guide us as we try to live as stewards within the integrity of creation.

environmental accounting

A type of accounting that attempts to include the value of the environment—which cannot be measured in dollars only—when making economic decisions.

Society's Role in Stewardship

Individual stewardship can do a lot (see the sidebar "Living as a Steward of the Earth"), but it will not be enough to sustain the earth for future generations. Our brief examination of ecological crises in article 42, "Our Relationship with Creation," illustrates that a web of interconnected social

Live It!

Living as a Steward of the Earth

As stewards each of us is called to do what we can to care for the earth. Here are some ways we can do this:

- Reduce consumption by bicycling, bussing, or carpooling instead of driving alone. Replace incandescent lights with compact fluorescent bulbs. Buy products that use less packaging and products you will be able to use for a long time. Buy used instead of new.
- Become educated about what can and cannot be recycled. If your community does not have a recycling program, lobby your city or county government for one. Buy recycled products.
- See what you can share with friends, neighbors, or siblings so that each person doesn't have to buy the same thing. Lawn mowers, cars, clothes, and tools are all possibilities.
- Support legislation that provides for good environmental stewardship. Check the Environmental Justice Program and the Catholic Coalition on Climate Change sponsored by the U.S. bishops.
- Evaluate the energy use of your home, school, or church. Most power companies offer to help homes and businesses reduce their energy consumption. Easy-to-implement advice can cut back on energy use by 10 to 30 percent.

sustainable development

A pattern of resource use that serves to meet human needs while also preserving natural resources to also meet the needs of future generations.

Through the use of environmentally friendly practices, such as the use of solar power, businesses can be better stewards of the environment.

structures contributes to these crises. To address these ecological crises, societies need to develop social structures that sustain the earth's natural environment for future generations, a practice called **sustainable development.**

Businesses and governments have an especially important role in these social changes because their actions can have a huge impact on the environment. Business and government leaders must weigh the contribution a society's economic activities make to the common good against the harm these activities cause the environment. Following are some examples of businesses' and governments' doing this.

Patagonia

Patagonia, a manufacturer of outdoor recreation equipment and clothing, is a good example of how companies can incorporate stewardship into their business practices. Their business statement is "Build the best product, cause no unnecessary harm, use business to inspire and implement solutions to the environmental crisis." The employees of Patagonia regularly evaluate the environmental impact of their products and adapt their business practices to be as environmentally friendly as possible. For instance, conventionally grown cotton uses many pesticides and toxic defoliants. So Patagonia began using pesticide-free organic cotton in its products. Their Common Threads Recycling Program encourages customers to return their worn-out garments so the company can recycle the materials into new clothing. (Patagonia Web site, 2010)

IKEA

IKEA, known for its furniture products, is another business committed to sustainable economic and environmentally friendly practices. The company has a commitment to reduce the energy consumption in all its stores by 25 percent through more efficient lighting, heating, and cooling, and through efficient trans-

© shutterstock/Lisa F. Young

portation. The company is working to certify that the wood and cotton used in its products come from forests and farms that use environmentally friendly and sustainable practices. (IKEA Web site, 2010)

California

The state of California is taking active steps to reduce its greenhouse gas emissions. The state recognizes that the potential climate change caused by increased greenhouse gases in the atmosphere will negatively affect its water supply, agriculture, fishing industry, and forests, so it is taking steps to significantly reduce its greenhouse gas emissions. It is doing this with a comprehensive strategy calling for more fuel-efficient and less-polluting vehicles and greater use of renewable energy sources. (California Climate Change Web site)

A Word of Hope

At the end of *Renewing the Earth*, the U.S. bishops acknowledge that working for environmental justice is very challenging, offering these encouraging words:

A just and sustainable society and world are not an optional ideal, but a moral and practical necessity. Without justice, a sustainable economy will be beyond reach. Without an ecologically responsible world economy, justice will be unachievable. To accomplish either is an enormous task; together they seem overwhelming. But "[a]ll things are possible" to those who hope in God (Mk 10:27). Hope is the virtue at the heart of a Christian environmental ethic. Hope gives us the courage, direction, and energy required for this arduous common endeavor. . . .

Saving the planet will demand long and sometimes sacrificial commitment. It will require continual revision of our political habits, restructuring economic institutions, reshaping society, and nurturing global community. But we can proceed with hope because, as at the dawn of creation, so today the Holy Spirit breathes new life into all earth's creatures. Today, we pray with new conviction and concern for all God's creation:

Send forth thy Spirit, Lord
and renew the face of the earth.

(14)

Sustainable development may not seem like a spiritual practice. But many people who are committed to it approach it as an important part of their spirituality. This is reinforced in the following teaching of the *Catechism*: "[Faith in God] *means making good use of created things*: faith in God, the only One, leads us to use everything that is not God only insofar as it brings us closer to him" (226). By being good stewards of the earth and its resources, we participate in God's perfection of creation and grow closer to him in the process. ✝

Part Review

1. What is meant by *integrity of creation?*

2. Describe some warning signs that humanity must better cultivate and care for creation.

3. What do the Creation accounts in Genesis teach us about our stewardship of creation?

4. What are the implications if we truly believe that creation is a gift for the common good?

5. What factors must be kept in mind to do a true environmental accounting when making business decisions?

6. Describe the role that businesses and governments can play in the stewardship of creation.

Living Justly

Part 1

Social Dimensions of the Beatitudes

Blessed are the poor in spirit,
  for theirs is the kingdom of
  heaven.

Blessed are they who mourn,
  for they will be comforted.

Blessed are the meek,
  for they will inherit the land.

Blessed are they who hunger and
  thirst for righteousness,
  for they will be satisfied.

Blessed are the merciful,
  for they will be shown mercy.

Blessed are the clean of heart,
  for they will see God.

Blessed are the peacemakers,
  for they will be called children of
  God.

Blessed are they who are persecuted
  for the sake of righteousness,
  for theirs is the kingdom of
  heaven.

(Matthew 5:3–10)

In the Gospel of Matthew, Jesus begins the Sermon on the Mount by proclaiming the Beatitudes, thus placing them at the heart of his moral teaching. The Beatitudes are the fulfillment of God's Covenant promises to Abraham. They teach us how to fulfill the longing for happiness that God has placed in every human heart. That longing will be completely fulfilled when we reach the final end to which God calls us, a destiny that has many names: our eternal rest in God, the beatific vision, the Kingdom of God, and Heaven. The Beatitudes teach us the actions and attitudes that are essential for a Christian life. Each article in this part is devoted to two beatitudes. After a short reflection on what each beatitude teaches us about the social dimension of the Gospel call, an example is given of a person or group that is a living model of this beatitude.

The articles in this part address the following topics:

^{Article}45 Becoming Poor in Spirit and Compassionate

Like all the Beatitudes, the first two direct us to look beyond ourselves and to focus instead on God and on the needs of his people. The first beatitude calls us to place our complete trust in God to provide for our needs. The second beatitude calls us to offer compassion and mercy to those who are suffering.

envy
Jealousy, resentment, or sadness because of another person's good fortune. It is one of the capital sins and contrary to the Tenth Commandment.

Blessed Are the Poor in Spirit, For Theirs Is the Kingdom of Heaven

The first beatitude does not mean that God wants people to live in poverty. Not having enough food to eat or clothes to wear or a place to live is an offense against human dignity. Rather, the first beatitude calls us to embrace spiritual poverty, which means placing our complete trust in God to provide for our needs. This is what Jesus teaches us when he says, "Take care to guard against all greed, for though one may be rich, one's life does not consist of possessions" (Luke 12:15).

Becoming poor in spirit is the way we live out the Tenth Commandment, "You shall not covet your neighbor's goods." The Tenth Commandment forbids the sin of greed that comes from a lust for wealth and the power that comes with it. It also forbids the sin of **envy**, which is the sadness we feel when someone has something we do not have and we are consumed with an unhealthy desire to have it for ourselves. To avoid these sins, we must have a spiritual detachment from material wealth so that we are free to choose a lifestyle that is not based on greed but rather on what will best contribute to the common good. Chris-

"Blessed are the poor in spirit." The Catholic Worker movement, founded in 1933 by Peter Maurin and Dorothy Day, is committed to the care of the poor. Have you ever visited a Catholic Worker house?

© Marquette University Archives

tians develop this detachment in many ways, all of which require goodwill, humility, and placing our faith in God to provide what we truly need to be happy. One important way is giving alms, or money, to those in need. This is a witness to human solidarity, a work pleasing to God. Another way is to be in solidarity with people who are poor or in need. We do this by spending time with them while engaging in works of charity and works of justice and by praying for them. In following the call to be poor in spirit, some Christians even commit themselves to voluntary poverty. They live very simple lives in order to devote themselves more fully to prayer, charitable actions, and justice.

The Catholic Worker Movement

Many Catholic organizations that exemplify the beatitude, "Blessed are the poor in spirit." The Catholic Worker movement is one of the few that began in the United States. It was founded in 1933 by Dorothy Day and Peter Maurin. Dorothy Day was a journalist, an unmarried mother, and a convert to Catholicism. In the Catholic faith, she found the answer to her heart's desire for meaning and happiness. Peter Maurin was a lifelong Catholic who was deeply committed to Catholic social teaching. He was a philosopher who believed that the true answer to society's social problems is a commitment to the basic values of the Gospel.

In the middle of the Great Depression, when the unemployment rate was nearly 25 percent and many families were struggling just to survive, Peter urged Dorothy to publish a newspaper promoting Catholic social teaching. They wanted to educate Catholics on social justice and encourage them to practice the works of mercy, and they wanted to support workers who were struggling to find meaningful work and just wages. The paper, called *Catholic Worker*, became very successful and soon people were donating food, clothing, money, and time. Dorothy then opened a house of hospitality to provide food and housing to homeless and hungry people.

The movement quickly spread and new Catholic Worker houses and Catholic Worker farms were started across the country. The Catholic Worker Web site reports that in 2010 there were over 185 Catholic Worker communities around the world, with 168 in the United States. Although each community is independent, they all do share some common commitments:

- **A commitment to the philosophy of personalism, which sees the freedom and dignity of every person as the basis for morality and all human actions** This stands in contrast to a self-centered individualism.
- **A commitment to radical nonviolence** Catholic Workers believe that violence must be fought with the "spiritual weapons of prayer, fasting and noncooperation with evil" (*Catholic Worker,* May 2008).
- **A commitment to living the works of mercy** Catholic Worker houses are communities devoted to feeding the hungry, clothing the naked, and sheltering the homeless.
- **A commitment to voluntary poverty** Catholic Worker volunteers live with the poor people they serve and depend on the charity of others. They live the spiritual truth that real happiness and meaning is found in detachment from material wealth.

Dorothy Day on Voluntary Poverty

In the fall of 1951, Dorothy Day wrote a letter to friends of the Catholic Worker asking for financial help. The letter is interesting because it is not filled with examples of desperate need but rather speaks about the wonder of how God provides so much with so little. It is an attitude of trust that is worth cultivating in our own lives!

"So much with so little," not "so little and so late." This has been running through my head as I thought of writing this appeal. It never ceases to amaze us, how through all these eighteen years we can keep on serving coffee, regardless of price, and soup and bread in so many of our farms throughout the land. . . .

We take what comes, and the Spanish saying, a baby is always born with a loaf of bread under its arm, is true. We have proved it in our Catholic Worker farms, houses of hospitality, and families, these many years. Voluntary poverty works. It is practical, and we have found it so by practicing it. Sometimes one feels it a joy and we do not have to remind ourselves to rejoice always. But there are moments also when it becomes appalling, when the pressure of people and human need becomes overwhelming. But one can take time out to sit on a park bench across the street and look at the children in the playground and pray and the burden lifts.

(In *Catholic Worker,* October 1951)

Blessed Are They Who Mourn, for They Will Be Comforted

consecrated life
A state of life recognized by the Church in which a person publicly professes vows of poverty, chastity, and obedience.

The second beatitude does not mean that God wants people to be perpetually sad; rather, he wants us to be compassionate. Why do people cry when they hear about another person's tragedy? It is because they are moved by compassion. God calls us to be compassionate, to be moved by the suffering and the needs of others and to be moved by the effects of sin and evil in the world. Our compassion must lead to action, whether that action is prayer, a work of charity, a work of justice, or all three. The comfort this beatitude promises as the result of compassion is knowing that in Heaven God will "wipe every tear from their eyes, and there shall be no more death or mourning, wailing or pain, [for] the old order has passed away" (Revelation 21:4).

Project Rachel

Project Rachel is a Catholic ministry to women and men whose lives have been touched by the loss of abortion. Its name comes from Scripture:

"Blessed are they who mourn." Through ministries such as Project Rachel, members of the Body of Christ reach out with compassion to those grieving from loss. Who in your life needs you to bring compassion and comfort to them?

> In Ramah is heard the sound of moaning,
> of bitter weeping!
> Rachel mourns her children,
> she refuses to be consoled
> because her children are no more.
> (Jeremiah 31:15)

The mothers and fathers of aborted children often experience sorrow, shame, and depression after the abortion is

performed. They find themselves grieving the death of their unborn baby. Sometimes this happens immediately, sometimes many years later. Often the abortion is a secret that they are ashamed to reveal. Project Rachel provides trained counselors who are available as compassionate, spiritual guides to help these individuals to express their grief and sorrow, to receive forgiveness (especially through the Sacrament of Penance and Reconciliation), and to find peace. This work is a living application of the second beatitude, "Blessed are they who mourn, for they will be comforted."

The members of Project Rachel know that every human being deserves to know God's compassion, forgiveness, and healing, especially those who have participated in a seriously evil act. One woman who has been supported by a Project Rachel counselor says: "I can now look at myself without seeing a lonely, selfish, desperate young woman. I see a woman who has grieved the loss of a baby and mourned the part of myself which died along with the baby. Someone was there to help pick up the pieces of my broken life and help me move on." Project Rachel shows the world that justice and mercy must walk hand-in-hand. ✝

evangelical counsels

The call to go beyond the minimum rules of life required by God (such as the Ten Commandments and the precepts of the Church) and strive for spiritual perfection through a life marked by a commitment to chastity, poverty, and obedience.

The Vow of Poverty

The vow of poverty is one of the three vows made by those who are called to the **consecrated life**. The vows are the public expression to live "the **evangelical counsels** of poverty, chastity, and obedience, in a stable state of life recognized by the Church" (CCC, 944). The most common form of the consecrated life is the religious communities of priests, brothers, and sisters found throughout the world. Those living a consecrated life seek to live the first beatitude in a deep and profound way.

What this means practically is that all the members of a religious community share their finances together. For members who work outside the community, instead of receiving an individual paycheck for their work or ministry, the paycheck goes to the community. From their community they receive a living allowance for their basic needs: food, housing, clothing, transportation, and so on. Sometimes the religious community engages in a shared enterprise to support the community, such as making wine or jelly, but the proceeds of their work go to the community, not to individuals. This is a powerful witness to the social justice principle of solidarity.

46 Becoming Meek and Thirsting for Righteousness

When we follow Jesus' call to be meek and to thirst for righteousness, expressed in the third and fourth beatitudes, we become more willing to sacrifice our own comfort for the good of others. By doing this we ensure that not only we but others too are treated with dignity and respect, as beloved children of God.

Blessed Are the Meek, For They Will Inherit the Land

Meek is defined as (1) "enduring injury with patience and without resentment,"(2) "deficient in spirit and courage," and (3) "not violent or strong." We can be sure that in the third beatitude Jesus is calling us to endure hardship with patience and without resentment; however, he is not calling us to be cowardly or weak, as the definitions might suggest. As we work for justice, we will encounter frustrations and hard-ships. We will even sometimes be attacked and our character questioned. The third beatitude calls us to endure these hard-ships with perseverance and strength. It calls us to respond to personal attacks with gentleness and forgiveness so that we do not become arrogant and violate other people's dignity.

African-American Nonviolent Civil Rights Movement

The Civil Rights movement in the 1950s and 1960s may seem like ancient history to teens today. But these years must be remembered, because they have some of the saddest and some of the proudest moments in U.S. history. They were sad times because of the extreme prejudice and hatred displayed by many white citizens toward people of color. But these years are also a proud moment in U.S. history because of the courage and the faith shown by the Christians involved in the Civil Rights movement. These people lived the third beatitude, "Blessed are the meek."

Inspired by the preaching of Christian leaders like Martin Luther King Jr., many of the people in the Civil Rights movement committed themselves to standing up to civil rights abuses with nonviolent love. At the start of the Civil Rights movement, in the 1950s, it was illegal for a black person to sit on the "white" side of the bus or go to a "white"

Thomas Merton on Nonviolence

The Civil Rights movement shows us how the beatitude of meekness can be lived out through nonviolent resistance to sinful social structures. The well-known Catholic spiritual writer and monk Thomas Merton wrote several essays on the spirituality of nonviolent resistance during these years. Reflect on these powerful words from his essay "Blessed Are the Meek," published in 1967:

> This aspect of Christian nonviolence is extremely important and it gives us the key to a proper understanding of the meekness which accepts being "without strength" not out of masochism, quietism, defeatism, or false passivity, but trusting in the strength of the Lord of truth. Indeed, we repeat, Christian nonviolence is nothing if not first of all a formal profession of faith in the Gospel message that the *Kingdom has been established* and that the Lord of truth is indeed risen and reigning over his Kingdom.

> Faith of course tells us that we live in a time of eschatological struggle, facing a fierce combat which marshals all the forces of evil and darkness against the still-invisible truth, yet this combat is already *decided* by the victory of Christ over death and over sin. The Christian can renounce the protection of violence and risk being humble, therefore vulnerable, not because he trusts in the supposed efficacy of a gentle and persuasive tactic that will disarm hatred and tame cruelty, but because he believes that the hidden power of the Gospel is demanding to be manifested in and through his own poor person.

> (Reprinted from Thomas Merton, *Faith And Violence*, page 18)

school in many states. People active in the Civil Rights movement confronted this prejudice and discrimination without resorting to violence. When violence was inflicted on them, they responded with love and strength—the meekness of the beatitude.

Some of the most powerful exercises of nonviolence during those years were the Montgomery bus boycott, the student sit-ins, and freedom rides. The Montgomery bus boycott started in 1955 after Rosa Parks was arrested for refusing to give up her seat to make room for a white passenger. The boycott lasted over a year until a federal court ordered the buses to be desegregated. In 1960 in Greensboro, North Carolina, four black students sat down at a segregated lunch counter and refused to leave. This inspired similar nonviolent protests against segregation by students across the country. The Freedom Riders were groups of people who traveled across the country in the 1960s, purposely ignoring the segregated bus seating, bathrooms, drinking fountains, and waiting rooms. These are just some examples of the many people of faith who worked for justice in the Civil Rights movement. They brought an end to the blatant prejudice and discrimination in U.S. society by bravely enduring hardships without violent retaliation. They showed society what it means to be meek while remaining spiritually strong.

© Bettmann/CORBIS

"Blessed are the meek." Leaders such as Martin Luther King Jr. show us that being meek does not mean being cowardly or weak.

Blessed Are They Who Hunger and Thirst for Righteousness, for They Will Be Satisfied

In the Bible a righteous person is someone who is truthful, merciful, just, and compassionate. He or she is a person of holiness who is in right relationship with God and other people. The fourth beatitude calls us to want to be this type of person as much as a starving person wants food. A righteous person will naturally develop a social conscience and will work to help society become more truthful, merciful, just, and compassionate. Our hunger to be righteous people and our hunger for society to be righteous will be fully satisfied when we reach our eternal reward.

A Changed Life

Abdoulai is a Nigerian man who knows the hunger for righteousness. His life was transformed, partly through a development program sponsored by Catholic Relief Services. Abdoulai's family lived in extreme poverty. In early 2010 his family was forced to eat weeds to survive. The rainy season was so bad in 2009 that his crops did not produce even one sack of grain. The food didn't last a week. Without enough food, Abdoulai and his family began to experience the symptoms of starvation: blurred vision, time disorientation, and psychological depression.

© Lane Hartill/Catholic Relief Services

"Blessed are those who hunger and thirst for righteousness." To thirst for righteousness includes the desire to live a life committed to justice. Where in your life and in the world are you being called to work for justice?

Then Catholic Relief Services (CRS) showed up in his village. Through the contributions of compassionate Catholics throughout the United States, CRS funds hundreds of projects around the world that foster human and economic development in poverty stricken areas. One of the projects is building a berm, or a small wall, around a plain that used to be a forest near Abdoulai's village. The berm will help trap rainwater, giving grass and other plants a chance to grow, transforming the barren plain into a green field. Abdoulai was offered a job building the berm. He is doing hard labor in 115-degree weather and making only $3.50 a day, but it is more money than he has ever made before, enough to buy food for his family at the local market. "I had a lot of stress before," he says, "but now food is not a problem. Now we have leftovers."

Abdoulai's story is an example of how true development responds to the hunger for righteousness. In his poverty Abdoulai saw no hopeful future for himself or his family. The human and economic development offered by CRS gives him hope for a different future. The people who donate to CRS do so because of their hunger to see righteousness restored to those who lack it. And those who receive the development aid see their hunger for righteousness met through the development provided to build a life of greater dignity for their families and their communities. ✞

^{Article} 47 Becoming Merciful and Pure of Heart

Because of the effects of Original Sin, we are all prone to making sinful choices—choices that contradict God's will for us. Sometimes those sinful choices visibly harm others, and sometimes the damage done is more difficult to recognize. The fifth beatitude calls us to be forgiving when others' actions hurt us, and to ask forgiveness when we hurt others. The sixth beatitude calls us to seek God's help in being "pure of heart," and to avoid the harm brought to ourselves and to others when we violate the Sixth and Ninth Commandments.

Blessed Are the Merciful, for They Will Be Shown Mercy

The fifth beatitude teaches a value found throughout the Gospels. Through such examples as telling Peter to forgive "not seven times but seventy-seven times" (Matthew 18:22) and the Parable of the Prodigal Son (see Luke 15:11–32), Jesus emphasized the necessity of mercy and forgiveness in the Christian life. Forgiveness and mercy are part of the prayer he taught his followers, "forgive us our debts, / as we forgive our debtors" (Matthew 6:12). Christ calls us to be quick to ask for forgiveness and quick to extend forgiveness to others.

Forgiveness and mercy are also important as social values. Groups and nations must also ask for forgiveness and extend forgiveness after conflicts. Without the reconciliation that is brought about by forgiveness and mercy, human beings will typically perpetuate the spiral of violence (see article 31, "The Causes of Violence"). Without reconciliation we hold grudges, which can cause bitterness and lead to future acts of injustice. So even though asking others for forgiveness and giving our forgiveness might be difficult, it is not optional. If we are not merciful ourselves, we cannot expect to receive mercy.

Pope Saint John Paul II

On May 13, 1981, in Saint Peter's Square, as Pope Saint John Paul II entered an open car to greet pilgrims, a trained sniper took aim and shot him. The sniper was captured by the

Vatican security chief, a nun, and several spectators in the crowd. The sniper's name was Mehmet Ali Agca.

Saint John Paul II suffered the loss of three-quarters of his blood, and underwent five hours of emergency surgery. The Pope later credited his survival to the intervention of Our Lady of Fatima, whose feast day is on May 13, the day of the shooting.

When Saint John Paul II regained consciousness, he immediately pardoned Agca. Two years later, on December 27, 1983, the Pope visited Agca in prison. There he forgave him in person, in the midst of a long conversation in the corner of Agca's cell. At the Pope's request, Agca was pardoned for his crime in Italy, then extradited to Turkey, his home country, where he served ten more years for a previous murder. He was released from prison in 2010.

Pray It!

A Prayer for Mercy

God of Compassion,
You let your rain fall on the just and the unjust.
Expand and deepen our hearts
so that we may love as You love,
even those among us
who have caused the greatest pain by taking life.
For there is in our land a great cry for vengeance
as we fill up death row and kill the killers
in the name of justice, in the name of peace.
Jesus, our brother,
you suffered execution at the hands of the state
but you did not let hatred overcome you.
Help us to reach out to victims of violence
so that our enduring love may help them heal.
Holy Spirit of God,
You strengthen us in the struggle for justice,
Help us to work tirelessly
for the abolition of state-sanctioned death
and to renew our society in its very heart
so that violence will be no more.
Amen.

(Sr. Helen Prejean)

"Blessed are the merciful." Forgiveness and mercy often go hand in hand. Who in your life is in need of your forgiveness and mercy? From whom do you need to seek forgiveness?

© Gianni Giansanti/Sygma/Corbis

In his act of merciful forgiveness, Saint John Paul II was a powerful witness to the fifth beatitude and conveyed an important message to all Christians—indeed to all the world: even in the face of hatred and sin, mercy and forgiveness are absolutely necessary. It is only by showing mercy that we will know mercy.

Blessed Are the Clean Of Heart, For They Will See God

The sixth beatitude can best be understood in light of another passage from the Gospel of Matthew: "But the things that come out of the mouth come from the heart, and they defile. For from the heart come evil thoughts, murder, adultery, unchastity, theft, false witness, blasphemy" (15:18–19). In Jesus' time the heart was not just considered the seat of the emotions but the location of our conscience and moral decision making, which is why Jesus taught that an unclean heart leads to sin. A sinful person is not in right relationship with God and will be unable to "see God."

The sixth beatitude calls us to desire to be holy people— people who are charitable, who are chaste, and who embrace God's truth. In particular, the sixth beatitude is connected to the Ninth Commandment, "You shall not covet your neighbor's wife." This commandment warns us against the dangers of sexual lust (also called carnal concupiscence). When our hearts are not clean, we are more easily tempted by sexual lust. The struggle to keep our hearts pure can be thought of us a spiritual battle. Properly forming our conscience, being chaste in our dress and actions, practicing the virtue of **temperance,** praying regularly, and frequently receiving the Eucharist and the Sacrament of Penance and Reconciliation are our chief weapons in our battle against lust and sexual sin.

temperance
The cardinal virtue by which one moderates his or her appetites and passions to achieve balance in the use of created goods.

The Battle for a Pure Heart

Dominic (not his real name) first started using pornography when he was twelve years old. He found a hidden stack of magazines and was very quickly hooked on the images he saw. When he got his own computer in his bedroom, he would search for pornography almost every night. Dominic knew this was wrong and felt ashamed, but when he tried to quit, it would only last for a few days or weeks and then the temptation was too great and he was using pornography again.

Modesty in Society

The virtue of modesty often seems to be missing from our society. It seems that many people do not even know what modesty is. The simplest explanation is that modesty is the virtue of avoiding sexually explicit talk, sexually explicit images, and sexually explicit dress. It is an important way we protect our God-given holiness. It requires patience, decency, and good judgment. We practice modesty in what we wear, what we listen to, and what we watch so that we do not unnecessarily arouse our own sexual desires or the sexual desires of other people.

It is easy to be complacent about how we dress and what we watch and listen to today because we live in a society that encourages women, men, and even children to dress in sexually provocative ways and where sexual innuendo is frequently heard in music, movies, and everyday conversation. We must be strong in our conviction that society must change its values; we must not change ours. When more people request modest clothing styles, those styles will become more available, and suggestive or immodest clothing options will be lessened. When people ignore sexually explicit advertising and complain about it, it will be used less. Society can and will become more supportive of modesty if people of faith demand it.

This continued throughout high school and college, and eventually Dominic stopped going to church. When he met his future wife and got married, he thought that surely this would be the end of his problem. But it wasn't. When his wife caught him using pornography, she threatened to leave him if he didn't get help. So he talked to a priest. The priest was kind and understanding and told Dominic he had a spiritual problem that needed a spiritual solution. He recommended a support group to Dominic and told him to start coming to church again and to receive the Sacraments, starting with the Sacrament of Penance and Reconciliation.

Dominic did everything the priest recommended and more. The support group gave him the accountability he needed and friends who supported him in his struggle. He receives the Eucharist several times a week and the Sacrament of Penance and Reconciliation several times a month. Though it wasn't easy, especially at first, Dominic now has not used pornography in several years. And he feels a special call to support other men and women struggling with this sin in their lives. He counsels others who join the support group. He speaks to groups about the dangers of societal structures that support pornography and prostitution. Dominic has seen the promise of the sixth beatitude in his life and in the lives of others: "Blessed are the clean of heart, for they shall see God." ✝

© Bill.Wittman/www.wpwittman.com

"Blessed are the clean of heart." We are blessed to have the Sacraments to strengthen us in our efforts to become the holy people God calls us to be.

Part 2

Prayer and Action

This book's final part is perhaps the most crucial. The Church has a missionary mandate, a command from Jesus Christ to preach the Gospel to all people. In God's plan the Church is the sacrament of salvation for all people and all nations. Our work for justice and peace is part of that missionary mandate. This work requires perseverance and endurance because it is not a task that has an end, it is not a struggle that we will "win." Jesus himself said, "The poor you will always have with you" (Mark 14:7), indicating that the need for works of charity and works of justice will continue until the Last Judgment. So we must assume that action for justice and peace—in whatever ways God calls us to do this—is a lifelong task.

So this is the crucial question: How do we sustain ourselves to follow Christ's call for our entire life? Many young Catholics are enthusiastic about helping those in need and about working for justice. However, over time the enthusiasm often fades with the demands of work and raising a family. Making time for works of charity and justice becomes harder and harder. Little by little Catholics who were at one time dedicated to the Church's social teaching find themselves living just the same lifestyle as everyone else.

The challenge of sustaining a commitment to, and involvement in, working for justice is a spiritual one. It requires that we balance our outer life of work and action with an inner life of prayer. The articles in this part will help you to think about how our prayer and our action on behalf of the Gospel support each other. The emphasis in these articles is not on how to pray, a topic covered in other books in the Living in Christ series; rather, these articles emphasize the importance of taking time to pray, even in a busy life.

The articles in this part address the following topics:

Article 49 The Sabbath Challenge

Sabbath

In the Old Testament, the "seventh day," on which God rested after the work of Creation was completed. In the Old Law, the weekly day of rest to remember God's work through private prayer and communal worship. For Catholics, Sunday, the day on which Jesus was raised, which we are to observe with participation in the Eucharist in fulfillment of the Third Commandment.

The Third Commandment is a reminder about the importance of balancing action and prayer, although we might not always realize it. Many Catholics think that "Remember to keep holy the Lord's Day" is primarily a command to attend Mass on Sunday. But Sunday, the Lord's Day, has its roots in the Jewish practice of the **Sabbath.** The Sabbath is more than just a day; it is a spiritual truth about how God wants us to live. This article explores what we learn from Revelation about the Sabbath. By respecting these spiritual truths, we continually renew ourselves to live our Christian vocation.

The Biblical Origins of Sabbath

We first encounter the Sabbath principle in the first Creation account of Genesis. After God had finished his work in the six days of the Creation of the world, we are told: "Since on the seventh day God was finished with the work he had been doing, he rested on the seventh day from all the work he had

The Sabbath and the Lord's Day

As faithful Jews, Jesus and his disciples would have carefully observed the Sabbath. So why did the first Christians break from their tradition and begin to observe their holy day on Sunday? The reason is Jesus Christ's Resurrection. The Gospels carefully record that the Resurrection occurred sometime after the Sabbath day ended and by dawn on Sunday: "After the Sabbath, as the first day of the week was dawning, Mary Magdalene and the other Mary came to see the tomb" (Matthew 28:1).

Because of the Resurrection, Jesus' followers came to see Sunday not only as the first day of God's Creation of the world but also as the symbolic "first day" of the New Creation that begins with Christ's Resurrection. They began meeting on Sundays to celebrate the Eucharist in honor of Christ's command to "Do this in memory of me." Thus the first Christians moved the observance of the Sabbath from Saturday, the last day of the week, to Sunday, the day of the Resurrection, the first day of the New Creation.

Thus we call Sunday the Lord's Day in honor of our Lord and Savior, Jesus Christ. Christians also sometimes call Sunday the "eighth day," in recognition that with the Resurrection everything was changed; God had ushered in a new beginning in the history of salvation.

^{Article}

50 Jesus and Mary, Our Guides in Prayer and Action

Sometimes we think we are too busy to pray. Our lives are filled with school, work, connecting with friends, church activities, and family commitments. What time is left to pray?

When faced with these thoughts, it is wise to turn to the example of Jesus and his mother, Mary. Their lives were busy too. During the years of his public ministry, Jesus was constantly traveling, preaching, teaching, healing, and meeting with people who were curious about him and his message. As a peasant woman in ancient Israelite society, Mary would have had her days filled with planting, harvesting, preserving food, cooking, making clothes, and watching over Jesus and the other children of her extended family. Yet despite their busy lives, the Gospels reveal that **prayer** was an essential part of their lives.

prayer
Lifting up of one's mind and heart to God in praise, petition, thanksgiving, and intercession; communication with God in a relationship of love.

Jesus teaches us the importance of prayer through both his teachings and his actions.

Jesus, Our Model for Prayer

Most people are familiar with images of Jesus in action. The Gospels are filled with accounts of his travels, his proclamation of the Kingdom of God, his healing ministry, his teaching ministry, his formation of his disciples, his advocacy for justice, and his appearances after the Resurrection. What we might miss are the references to his prayer life.

Although all the Gospels have accounts of Jesus praying, the Gospel of Luke is sometimes called the Gospel of prayer because of its many references to prayer, particularly the prayer of Jesus. Let us consider the times and places that Luke portrays Jesus praying. He prays at the beginning of his ministry, immediately after being baptized (see Luke 3:21), and we can presume he prayed during his forty days in the desert (see 4:1–13). Luke also tells us that after busy periods of preaching and healing, Jesus would "withdraw to deserted places to pray" (5:16). Jesus prayed before or during important events in his ministry, such as before choosing the Apostles (see 6:12–13), before Peter confesses that he is

© Brooklyn Museum/Corbis

the Messiah (see 9:18–20), before the Transfiguration (see 9:28–29), before teaching his disciples to pray (see 11:1), and during the Last Supper (see 22:32).

Luke also notes how prayer prepared Jesus for the suffering of his Passion:

> After withdrawing about a stone's throw from them and kneeling, he prayed, saying, "Father, if you are willing, take this cup away from me; still, not my will but yours be done." [And to strengthen him an angel from heaven appeared to him. He was in such agony and he prayed so fervently that his sweat became like drops of blood falling on the ground.] (Luke 22:41–44)

What can we learn about the balance of prayer and action from the example of Jesus, our Master Teacher? We learn that prayer must precede any work we do for the Kingdom of God, because through prayer we place ourselves and our work in God's hands. We learn to take the time to pray in silence and solitude no matter how busy our day or week has been. We learn that getting through difficult and challenging times of life requires the prayerful submission of

The Justice Dimension of the Lord's Prayer

In the Gospel of Luke, when one of Jesus' disciples asks him to teach them to pray, Jesus responds by teaching the disciples the Lord's Prayer (see Luke 11:1–4). In just a few lines, this prayer provides a brilliant summary of the whole Gospel message, which is why the prayer Jesus taught is the perfect prayer of the Church. You may not realize that the Lord's Prayer also expresses some important justice themes. Here is a brief reflection on three lines:

Thy will be done on earth, as it is in heaven. Heaven is the fulfillment of the Kingdom of God, the "place" where God's perfect justice and peace reigns. We pray that the earth also become a place where mercy, compassion, justice, and peace reign.

Give us this day our daily bread. Notice that we pray that God give "us" our daily bread, not just give "me" my bread. The prayer emphasizes our solidarity with one another and that the earth's goods are meant for all people.

Forgive us our trespasses, as we forgive those who trespass against us. The prayer emphasizes the critical importance of forgiveness. Without forgiveness the spiral of injustice and violence continues.

The next time you pray the Lord's Prayer, remember that it includes petitions asking God to bring justice and peace into the world.

our will to the Father's will, following the example of Jesus. Prayer helps us to avoid cynicism (the belief that nothing will change) and hopelessness (the belief that nothing can change). Prayer nurtures us and helps us to avoid burn-out. Jesus persevered in his busy and challenging mission because he maintained his prayerful communion with his Father. We must do the same.

At his death, Christ's very last words were a prayer: "Father, into your hands I commend my spirit" (Luke 23:46). On the cross Jesus gives his very life, and in prayer he places this precious gift in his loving Father's hands for the salvation of the world.

> All the troubles, for all time, of humanity enslaved by sin and death, all the petitions and intercessions of salvation history are summed up in this cry of the incarnate Word. Here the Father accepts them and, beyond all hope, answers them by raising his Son. Thus is fulfilled and brought to completion the drama of prayer in the economy of creation and salvation. (*CCC*, 2606)

At Christ's death we see that his action and prayer are perfectly united. Our prayer and our action will also become united as we participate in Christ's mission and join our sacrifice to his. Let us pray to be true disciples of Christ, and let us become what we pray for.

In her prayer "May it be done to me according to your word" (Luke 1:38), Mary has given us a beautiful prayer for following God's will.

Mary's Prayer Is Yes to God

We know that Mary was a woman of action and prayer. Although the Gospels record only her famous prayer of praise (see the sidebar "Mary's *Magnificat*"), her prayerful life is revealed in other accounts about her in Scripture and Tradition.

At the Annunciation, when the angel Gabriel visits Mary to tell her she will bear the Son of God, she responds with the most simple and profound prayer in all of Scripture: "Behold, I am the handmaid of the Lord. May it be done to me according to your word" (Luke 1:38). In complete trust Mary says yes to God's will for her life. She is young, she is probably afraid, and she doesn't completely understand what all of this means. But Mary doesn't let any of these things stand in the way of giving herself completely to God in prayer and action.

Another example of Mary's attitude of prayer is the account of the wedding at Cana (see John 2:1–11). Jesus, his mother, and his disciples attend a wedding feast. During the celebration the wine runs out. Jesus has not yet performed his first miracle when Mary approaches him and says, "They have no wine" (John 2:3), clearly expecting Jesus to help. He responds that the time has not yet come for his ministry to begin. Undeterred, Mary tells the servers, "Do whatever he tells you" (John 2:5). This Gospel account instructs us in Mary's role as prayerful intercessor. Moved with compassion for all people in need, Mary intercedes with Jesus on their behalf just as she did at the wedding in Cana. Mary, as

Pray It!

Mary's Magnificat

Mary's prayer in the Gospel of Luke, called the *Magnificat*, is one of the most famous prayers in Catholic Tradition. In the Liturgy of the Hours, it is part of Evening Prayer (Vespers). As you pray this prayer, notice how its themes echo some of the Beatitudes and other themes in Catholic social teaching.

My soul proclaims the greatness of the Lord;
    my spirit rejoices in God my savior.
For he has looked upon his handmaid's lowliness;
    behold, from now on will all ages call me blessed.
The Mighty One has done great things for me,
    and holy is his name.
His mercy is from age to age
    to those who fear him.
He has shown might with his arm,
    dispersed the arrogant of mind and heart.
He has thrown down the rulers from their thrones
    but lifted up the lowly.
The hungry he has filled with good things;
    the rich he has sent away empty.
He has helped Israel his servant,
    remembering his mercy,
according to his promise to our fathers,
    to Abraham and to his descendants forever.
               (Luke 1:46–55)

the true Mother of God, *Theotokos* (a Greek word meaning "God-bearer"), is the best person to ask to pray for us. This is why the Church has a great devotion to Mary.

These accounts of Mary's prayer teach us two things about prayer and action. First, they teach us the importance of trusting in God, even when we do not understand all the implications of his call for our life. Saying yes to God's call in our prayer and in our actions will always be an act of faith. Second, Mary teaches us the importance of bringing the needs of others before God in prayer, in confidence that God will hear them. Mary is our spiritual Mother, and we can trust in her example and her love. We can ask her to join her prayers with our prayers. †

theological virtues
The name for the God-given virtues of faith, hope, and love. These virtues enable us to know God as God and lead us to union with him in mind and heart.

Empowered By Faith, Hope, and Love

God provides many gifts to help us follow the example of Jesus and Mary in living lives that are pleasing to God. Among the most important of those gifts are the **theological virtues** of faith, hope, and love. They are the foundation from which all human virtues flow. They are the source of energy for perfecting our relationship with God. *Theological* means "of the study of God." These virtues are theological because in accepting them and using them, we are drawn into deeper knowledge of and relationship with the Holy Trinity. Faith, hope, and love flow from God and back to him, providing a sort of "power loop" of divine energy that we can tap into through our faith. They give life and meaning to all the other virtues that are important in living a moral life.

Article 51 Ora et Labora

The famous Gospel account of Mary and Martha can be interpreted as a spiritual teaching on the importance of balancing work and action with prayer. Mary and Martha are sisters who Jesus comes to visit (see Luke 10:38–42). Martha busies herself with the work of hosting Jesus and his disciples while Mary sits at Jesus' feet, listening to his words. In exasperation, Martha complains to Jesus: "Lord, do you not care that my sister has left me by myself to do the serving? Tell her to help me" (verse 40). Jesus replies: "Martha, Martha, you are

© Erich Lessing / Art Resource, NY

The story of Martha and Mary (Luke 10:38–42) reminds us to balance work and prayer in our lives. How can you make prayer more a part of your life as a student?

anxious and worried about many things. There is need of only one thing. Mary has chosen the better part and it will not be taken from her" (verses 41–42).

In one sense Martha represents all Christians working hard in answer to God's call. Mary represents Christians in prayer, taking time to listen to God, to give him glory and to be nurtured by his presence. It is an easy temptation for us to be like Martha and get so caught up in our daily work that we neglect our relationship with God. Not that work is wrong. Notice that Jesus did not say that there was anything wrong with Martha's labors; rather, he corrects her by saying that work alone—even in service to him—is not enough. We must follow Mary's example and make nurturing our relationship with God through prayer and worship our first priority.

The balance of work and prayer is summarized in the Latin phrase *ora et labora,* which literally means "prayer and work" and has been a message to live by for Christians since the beginning of Western monasticism. This article briefly considers the origins of this phrase and what it has to teach us.

The Benedictine Rule

The origin of *ora et labora* can be traced to the beginnings of Western **monasticism.** Christian monasticism began in the third century when Christian men and women moved into the deserts of North Africa, Syria, and Palestine to retreat from the busyness of the world. They did this in order to develop a closer relationship with God in the silence of the wilderness. The first monks lived alone, as **hermits.** Many of these hermits developed reputations as wise spiritual counselors. It wasn't long, however, before communities were formed by people who wanted to experience the simplicity

monasticism

A form of Christian life followed by those who withdraw from ordinary life, and live alone or in community, in order to devote themselves to prayer and work in total dedication to God.

hermit

A person who lives a solitary life in order to commit himself or herself more fully to prayer and in some cases to be completely free for service to others.

The Rule of Saint Benedict

The Rule of Saint Benedict is a guide for living in monastic community. It gives guidelines for how the monks should pray, work, and behave. Even though it was written nearly fifteen hundred years ago, the rule's principles still apply today. Here is the chapter on daily labor. (Note that Prime, None, and Vespers are times of prayer—about 6 AM, early afternoon, and evening, respectively. In all, Benedict's rule identified eight times for daily prayer.)

Idleness is the enemy of the soul. Therefore the monks should be occupied at certain times in manual labor, and again at fixed hours in sacred reading. To that end we think that the times for each may be prescribed as follows.

From Easter until the Calends [first days] of October, when they come out from Prime in the morning let them labor at whatever is necessary until about the fourth hour, and from the fourth hour until about the sixth let them apply themselves to reading. After the sixth hour, having left the table, let them rest on their beds in perfect silence; or if anyone may perhaps want to read, let him read to himself in such a way as not to disturb anyone else. Let None be said rather early, at the middle of the eighth hour, and let them again do what work has to be done until Vespers.

And if the circumstances of the place or their poverty should require that they themselves do the work of gathering the harvest, let them not be discontented; for then are they truly monastics when they live by the labor of their hands, as did our Fathers and the Apostles. Let all things be done with moderation, however, for the sake of the faint-hearted.

(Adapted from *St. Benedict's Rule for Monasteries*, translated from the Latin by Leonard J. Doyle, pages 67–68)

of life in the wilderness but who did not want to live as hermits. The monastic movement then grew even more quickly.

Life in the first monastic communities could be quite unpredictable because individual monks sometimes became obsessed with strange or harsh practices. Wise leaders like Saint Basil (330–379) recognized that the practices of monastic life should not be determined by individual monks' ideas of what would lead to holiness. Basil and others developed rules for living in monastic communities. Basil's rules for monastic life stressed simple living: own almost nothing, eat only what is necessary, and obey the abbot of the monastery.

Over the next several hundred years, monastic communities continued to flourish and spread into Europe. A monk named Benedict started a monastery in Italy. Building on earlier monastic rules, he developed a new monastic rule—a detailed set of guidelines—that emphasized a simple, balanced, well-ordered life of work and prayer. The Rule of Saint Benedict eventually became the basic guide for the majority of monastic communities throughout the Western world. The rule is the basis for the popularity of the phrase *ora et labora*.

Benedict's insight about the spiritual benefits of a simple, balanced, well-ordered life of work and prayer is now an integral part of Christian spiritual practice. Members of Benedictine communities today still practice it as do many other religious communities. Similarly, many lay Christians have found the benefit of a regular daily routine of prayer and

Catholic Wisdom

The Saints on Prayer and Action

"Those prayers ascend quickly to God which the merits of our labors urge upon God."

(Cyprian of Carthage)

"Practice should be sustained by prayer, and prayer by practice."

(Pope Gregory the Great)

"The things, good Lord, that I pray for, give me the grace to labor for."

(Thomas More)

"How often I failed in my duty to God, because I was not leaning on a strong pillar of prayer."

(Teresa of Ávila)

evangelical counsels The call to go beyond the minimum rules of life required by God (such as the Ten Commandments and the Precepts of the Church) and strive for spiritual perfection through a life marked by a commitment to chastity, poverty, and obedience. *(page 235)*

excommunication A severe penalty that results from grave sin against Church law. The penalty is either imposed by a Church official or happens automatically as a result of the offense. An excommunicated person is not permitted to celebrate or receive the Sacraments. *(page 136)*

F

fair trade An organized social movement and market-based approach that aims to help producers in developing countries to obtain living wages for their labor. *(page 71)*

Fall, the Also called the Fall from grace, the biblical revelation about the origins of sin and evil in the world, expressed figuratively in the account of Adam and Eve in Genesis. *(page 12)*

fornication Sexual intercourse between a man and a woman who are not married. It is morally wrong to engage in intercourse before Marriage, a sin against the Sixth Commandment. *(page 178)*

free market A market system in which individuals and businesses are free to create and sell whatever goods and services they wish to sell at whatever price they wish to charge. *(page 207)*

G

genocide The systematic and planned extermination of an entire ethnic, religious, political, or cultural group of people. *(page 10)*

grace The free and undeserved gift of God's loving and active presence in the universe and in our lives, empowering us to respond to his call and to live as his adopted sons and daughters. Grace restores our loving communion with the Holy Trinity, lost through sin. *(page 26)*

H

hermit A person who lives a solitary life in order to commit himself or herself more fully to prayer and in some cases to be completely free for service to others. *(page 262)*

I

immigration, immigrant The movement of a person or a group of people to a new country, usually to take up permanent residence. The opposite of immigration is emigration, the movement of people out of a country. An immigrant is a person who has moved to take up residence in another country. *(page 186)*

infrastructures The basic facilities, services, and physical systems needed for the functioning of a community or society. Examples include public education, transportation, water supply, and energy supply systems. *(page 197)*

integrity of creation The way creation's many interdependent relationships fit together as a harmonious whole. *(page 215)*

J

just wage A salary that recognizes the value of the work being performed and that is high enough to allow the laborer and his or her immediate family to live a life of human dignity. Minimally, this means a wage above the poverty line. *(page 200)*

just war War involves many evils, no matter the circumstances. For a war to be just, it must be declared by a lawful authority, there must be just cause and the right intention (such as self-defense), and weapons must be used in a way that protects the lives of innocent people. *(page 160)*

justice The cardinal virtue concerned with the rights and duties within relationships; the commitment, as well as the actions and attitudes that flow from the commitment, to ensure that all persons—particularly people who are poor and oppressed—receive what is due them. *(page 56)*

L

labor Human work. *(page 201)*

Last Judgment The judgment of the human race by Jesus Christ at his second coming, as noted in the Nicene Creed. It is also called the Final Judgment. *(page 249)*

legal justice The social responsibilities that citizens owe their country and society. *(page 58)*

legitimate defense The teaching that limited violence is morally acceptable in defending yourself or your nation from an attack. *(page 159)*

lust Intense and uncontrolled desire for sexual pleasure. It is one of the seven capital sins. *(page 178)*

M

Magisterium The Church's living teaching office, which consists of all bishops, in communion with the Pope. *(page 55)*

masturbation Self-manipulation of one's sexual organs for the purpose of erotic pleasure or to achieve orgasm. It is a sin against the Sixth Commandment because the act cannot result in the creation of new life and because God created sexuality not for self-gratification but to unify a husband and wife in Marriage. *(page 178)*

migration, migrant The movement of a person or a group of people from one place to another. A migrant moves from one place to another without establishing a permanent residence. *(page 186)*

monasticism A form of Christian life followed by those who withdraw from ordinary life, and live alone or in community, in order to devote themselves to prayer and work in total dedication to God. *(page 262)*

mortal sin An action so contrary to the will of God that it results in complete separation from God and his grace. As a consequence of that separation, the person is condemned to eternal death. For a sin to be a mortal sin, three conditions must be met: the act must involve grave matter, the person must have full knowledge of the evil of the act, and the person must give his or her full consent in committing the act. *(page 84)*

N

natural law The natural law expresses the original moral sense that God gave us that enables us to discern by our intellect and reason what is good and what is evil. It is rooted in our desire for God, and is our participation in his wisdom and goodness because we are created in his divine likeness. *(page 84)*

New Law Divine Law revealed in the New Testament through the life and teaching of Jesus Christ and through the witness and teaching of the Apostles. The New Law perfects the Old Law and brings it to fulfillment. Also called the Law of Love. *(page 19)*

nonviolent resistance To confront injustice and violence with love, using only nonviolent strategies in working for justice and peace. *(page 173)*

O

Old Law Divine Law revealed in the Old Testament, summarized in the Ten Commandments. Also called the Law of Moses. It is succeeded by the New Law of the Gospels. *(page 19)*

original holiness The original state of human beings in their relationship with God, sharing in the divine life in full communion with him. *(page 11)*

original justice The state of complete harmony of our first parents with themselves, with each other, and with all of creation. *(page 11)*

Original Sin The sin by which the first human disobeyed God and thereby lost original holiness and became subject to death. Original Sin is transmitted to every person born into the world, except Mary and Jesus. *(page 13)*

P

Paschal Mystery The work of salvation accomplished by Jesus Christ mainly through his Passion, death, Resurrection, and Ascension. *(page 21)*

polygamy Having more than one spouse, an act contrary to the dignity of marriage and a sin against the Sixth Commandment. *(page 178)*

pornography A written description or visual portrayal of a person or action that is created or viewed with the intention of stimulating sexual feelings. Creating or using pornography is a sin against the Sixth and Ninth Commandments. *(page 178)*

prayer Lifting up one's mind and heart to God in praise, petition, thanksgiving, and intercession; communication with God in a relationship of love. *(page 257)*

prophet A person God chooses to speak his message of salvation. In the Bible, primarily a communicator of a divine message of repentance to the Chosen People, not necessarily a person who predicted the future. *(page 36)*

R

racism Treating people of a different race without the full respect their equal dignity requires. *(pages 53, 181)*

refugee Any person who seeks protection in another country because of war or natural disaster or because of a well-founded fear of persecution in his or her native land. *(page 191)*

reparation Making amends for something one did wrong that caused harm to another person or led to loss. *(page 121)*

restitution Making things right with another person or people who have been harmed by an injustice, or returning or replacing what rightfully belongs to another. *(page 121)*

S

Sabbath In the Old Testament, the "seventh day," on which God rested after the work of Creation was completed. In the Old Law, the weekly day of rest to remember God's work through private prayer and communal worship. For Catholics, Sunday, the day on which Jesus was raised, which we are to observe with participation in the Eucharist in fulfillment of the Third Commandment. *(page 252)*

salvation history The pattern of specific salvific events in human history in which God clearly reveals his presence and saving actions. Salvation was accomplished once and for all through Jesus Christ, a truth foreshadowed and revealed throughout the Old Testament. *(page 15)*

scandal An action or attitude—or the failure to act—that leads another person into sin. *(page 166)*

Scripture(s) Generally, the term for any sacred writing. For Christians, the Old and New Testaments that make up the Bible and are recognized as the Word of God. *(page 15)*

sexism Treating people of one gender without the full respect their equal dignity requires. *(page 179)*

politics and, 111
on poverty, 72, 200
on racism, 184–185
on rights and responsibilities, 69
social doctrine of the Church and,
    51–54
on solidarity, 77
on stewardship, 80, 223
on sustainability, 222
on themes of social justice teach-
    ing, 61
on wages, 200

V

Vatican Council II, 27, 48, 114–115,
    130, 164, 212
vengefulness, 33, 154, 170, 246. *see
    also* spiral of violence
violence. *see also* nonviolence; war,
    causes of, 151–157
    Fifth Commandment and, 150
    peace and, 167
    respect and, 62, 176
    sins and, 83
    spiral of, 152, 154–157, 166, 168,
        171–172, 240, 258
    U.S. and, 54
virtues, 56–57, 261
voting, 111, 112, 184
vulnerable people. *see also* poverty
    capitalism and, 210
    Catholic Worker movement and, *85*
    culture of death and, 129
    greater need of, 70
    Jesus' teachings, 43–44
    Missionaries of Charity and, *35*
    prophets on, 36–37
    sexual slave trade and, 180
    slavery and, 122
    solidarity and, 76
    USCCB on, 54

W

wages
    businesses and, 121, 200–201
    Catholic Worker and, 232
    1800s and, 45
    fair trade and, 71
    families and, 204
    food industry and, 74
    gap in U.S., 199
    Saint John XXIII on, 68

Leo XIII on, 46
prophets and, 37
rights to, 206
structures of sin and, 89, 92, 103
USCCB on, 75
U.S. laws and, 179, 211
war. *see also* violence; weapons
    age of, 181
    causes of, 150
    genocide and, 10
    human cost of, 161
    immigration and, 191
    just, 160
    migration and, 189
    self defense and, 157–159
    social structures and, 103
wealth. *see also* goods, material; greed;
    materialism
    businesses and, 121
    capitalism and, 210
    gap in, 199–201
    immigration and, 190
    Jesus' teachings, 23, 40–41, 231
    morality and, 47
    New Law and, 22
    Paul VI on, 49
    Pius XI on, 48
    poverty and, 196
    prophets on, 37
    saints on, 59
    social justice and, 14, 34
    solidarity and, 76
    success and, 210
weapons
    arms race, 161–164
    arms trade, 164–165
    blood diamonds and, 246
    common good and, 120
    of mass destruction, *162*, 163, 164
    nuclear, 48, 52, 53, 120, *157*,
        161–165
wedding at Cana, 250–251
Welch, Bud, 148
witnessing, 26
women, 48, 205
Women of Liberia for Peace, 245–247
words, 84, 97
work. *see* labor
workers' rights, 68, 72–75, 206
works of charity and justice, 99–103
World Peace Days, 223
worship, right to, 67

Acknowledgments

Scripture texts used in this work are taken from the *New American Bible, revised edition* © 2010, 1991, 1986, 1970 Confraternity of Christian Doctrine, Inc., Washington, D.C. All Rights Reserved. No part of this work may be reproduced or transmitted in any form or by any means, electronic or mechanical, including photocopying, recording, or by any information storage and retrieval system, without permission in writing from the copyright owner.

The quotations in this book labeled *Catechism* and *CCC* are from the English translation of the *Catechism of the Catholic Church* for use in the United States of America, second edition. Copyright © 1994 by the United States Catholic Conference, Inc.—Libreria Editrice Vaticana (LEV). English translation of the *Catechism of the Catholic Church: Modifications from the Editio Typica* copyright © 1997 by the United States Catholic Conference, Inc.—LEV.

The statistic on page 10 is from the History Place Web site, at *www.historyplace.com/worldhistory/genocide/index.html.*

The first excerpt on page 24 is from *God Is Love (Deus Caritas Est)*, number 22, at *www.vatican.va/holy_father/benedict_xvi/encyclicals/documents/hf_ben-xvi_enc_20051225_deus-caritas-est_en.html.* Copyright © 2005 LEV. Used with permission of LEV.

The second excerpt on page 24 is from *On Christian Hope (Spe Salvi)*, number 14, at *www.vatican.va/holy_father/benedict_xvi/encyclicals/documents/hf_ben-xvi_enc_20071130_spe-salvi_en.html.* Copyright © 2007 LEV. Used with permission of LEV.

The excerpt on page 27 is from *Decree on Ecumenism (Unitatis Redintegratio,* 1964), number 12, at *www.vatican.va/archive/hist_councils/ii_vatican_council/documents/vat-ii_decree_19641121_unitatis-redintegratio_en.html.* Copyright © LEV. Used with permission of LEV.

The excerpt on page 29 is from "General Audience," December 19, 2007, at *www.vatican.va/holy_father/benedict_xvi/audiences/2007/documents/hf_ben-xvi_aud_20071219_en.html.* Copyright © 2007 LEV. Used with permission of LEV.

The excerpt on pages 38–39 is from "Message of the Holy Father Pope John Paul II for the VIII World Youth Day," number 5, at *www.vatican.va/holy_father/john_paul_ii/messages/youth/documents/hf_jp-ii_mes_15081992_viii-world-youth-day_en.html.* Copyright © LEV. Used with permission of LEV.

The excerpts on pages 45, 106, 122, 125, 165, 166, and 208; the quotations on pages 50, 169–170, and 186; and the adapted bullet points on page 117 are from *Compendium of the Social Doctrine of the Church*, presentation page, numbers 168, 353, 415, 511, 516, and 353; presentation page,

517, and 431; and 426, respectively, by LEV (Washington, DC: United States Conference of Catholic Bishops [USCCB], 2005). English translation copyright © 2004 LEV. Used with permission of the USCCB.

The excerpts on pages 46 and 201 and the two quotations on page 209 are from *On the Condition of Labor* (*Rerum Novarum*, 1891), numbers 3, 20, 15, and 15, respectively, at *www.vatican.va/holy_father/leo_xiii/ encyclicals/documents/hf_l-xiii_enc_15051891_rerum-novarum_en.html*. Copyright © LEV. Used with permission of LEV.

The quotation on page 54 is from "Confronting a Culture of Violence: A Catholic Framework for Action," by the USCCB, at *www.usccb.org/sdwp/ national/criminal/ccv94.shtml*. Copyright © USCCB, Washington, D.C. All rights reserved.

The quotation on page 58 and the excerpts on pages 199 and 200 are from *Economic Justice for All : Pastoral Letter on Catholic Social Teaching and the U.S. Economy* (Washington, DC: USCCB, 1986), numbers 70, 185, and 196, respectively. Copyright © 1986 by the USCCB, Washington, D.C. All rights reserved. Used with permission of the USCCB. No part of this work may be reproduced or transmitted in any form or by any means, electronic or mechanical, including photocopying, recording, or by any information storage and retrieval system, without permission in writing from the copyright holder.

The quotation on page 61 and the excerpts on pages 64, 66, 69, 72, 75, 77, and 80 are from *Sharing Catholic Social Teaching: Challenges and Directions: Reflections of the U.S. Catholic Bishops,* by the USCCB, at *www. usccb.org/sdwp/projects/socialteaching/socialteaching.shtml*. Copyright © by the USCCB, Washington, D.C. All rights reserved. Used with permission of the USCCB. No part of this work may be reproduced or transmitted in any form or by any means, electronic or mechanical, including photocopying, recording, or by any information storage and retrieval system, without permission in writing from the copyright holder.

The quotation and the excerpts on page 73 are from *On Human Work* (*Laborem Exercens*), numbers 6, 25, and 27, respectively, at *www.vatican. va/holy_father/john_paul_ii/encyclicals/documents/hf_jp-ii_enc_14091981_ laborem-exercens_en.html*. Copyright © LEV. Used with permission of LEV.

The quotations on pages 75 and 76, the bullet points on page 76, and the numbered points and quotation on page 93 are quoted and adapted from *On Social Concern (Solicitudo Rei Socialis)*, numbers 38, 39, and 36–37, respectively, at *www.vatican.va/holy_father/john_paul_ii/ encyclicals/documents/hf_jp-ii_enc_30121987_solicitudo-rei-socialis_ en.html*. Copyright © LEV. Used with permission of LEV.

The quotations on pages 77, 159, 164, and 171 and the excerpts on pages 114–115 and 130 are from *Pastoral Constitution on the Church in the Modern World* (*Gaudium et Spes*, 1965), numbers 26, 79, 81, 78, 76, and 27, respectively, at *www.vatican.va/archive/hist_councils/ii_vatican_council/ documents/vat-ii_cons_19651207_gaudium-et-spes_en.html*. Copyright © LEV. Used with permission of LEV.

The "Pray It!: Social Justice Examination of Conscience" sidebar on page 79 is adapted from "Supplementary Questions to Examine Conscience in Light of Catholic Social Teaching," by the USCCB, at *www. usccb.org/sdwp/projects/socialteaching/examine/shtml*. Copyright © by the USCCB, Washington, D.C. All rights reserved. Used with permission of the USCCB.

The statistics on page 83 are from the Bread for the World Web site, at *www.bread.org/hunger/global/facts.html*.

The excerpt from the essay on page 85 was found at the Catholic Worker Web site, at *www.catholicworker.org/roundtable/easyessays.cfm*.

The quotations on pages 88 and 90 are from *Reconciliation and Penance*, number 16, at *www.vatican.va/holy_father/john_paul_ii/apost_ exhortations/documents/hf_jp-ii_exh_02121984_reconciliatio-et-paenitentia_en.html*. Copyright © LEV.

The excerpt on page 94 is quoted from *Community Service and Social Responsibility in Youth*, by James Youniss and Miranda Yates (Chicago: University of Chicago Press, 1977), page 65. Copyright © 1997 the University of Chicago.

The quotations on pages 96 and 97 are from *A Call to Action (Octogesima Adveniens)*, numbers 48 and 50, at *www.vatican.va/holy_father/ paul_vi/apost_letters/documents/hf_p-vi_apl_19710514_octogesima-adveniens_en.html*. Copyright © LEV. Used with permission of LEV.

The quotation on page 100 is from *Summa Theologica*, Question 66, 7, at *www.newadvent.org/summa/3066.htm*.

The quotations on pages 107, 108, and 109 and the excerpt on page 108 are from *Peace on Earth (Pacem in Terris)*, numbers 56, 63, 64, 137, and 88–89, respectively, at *www.vatican.va/holy_father/john_xxiii/ encyclicals/documents/hf_j-xxiii_enc_11041963_pacem_en.html*. Copyright © LEV. Used with permission of LEV.

The prayer on page 111 is reprinted from *Catholic Household Blessings and Prayers*, revised edition, by the USCCB (Washington, DC: USCCB, 2007), pages 372–373, found at *www.usccbpublishing.org/client/client_pdfs/ prayeraft.pdf*. Used with permission of Cardinal Adam Maida, Archdiocese of Detroit.

The excerpts on pages 120, 196, 198, 209–210, and 219 are from Pope John Paul II's *Hundredth Year (Centesimus Annus)*, numbers 43, 46, 52, 42, and 37, respectively, at *www.vatican.va/holy_father/john_paul_ii/ encyclicals/documents/hf_jp-ii_enc_01051991_centesimus-annus_en.html*. Copyright © LEV. Used with permission of LEV.

The excerpts on pages 130–131, 132, 133, 141, 143, 145–146, and 159 and the quotations on pages 134 and 143 are from *The Gospel of Life*

The information in the chart on page 161 is taken from "Deaths in Wars and Conflicts in the 20th Century," 3rd edition, by Milton Leitenberg, at the Cornell University Peace Studies Program Web site, at *www.einaudi.cornell.edu/peaceprogram/publications/occasional.asp*. Copyright © 2003, 2005, 2006 by Milton Leitenberg.

The quotations about landmines on page 163 are from "Catholic Campaign to Ban Landmines," by the USCCB, at *www.usccb.org/sdwp/international/landmine/brochure.shtml*. Copyright © USCCB, Washington, D.C. All rights reserved.

The statistics on page 164 are from "World Military Spending," by Anup Shah, at *www.globalissues.org/article/75/world-military-spending*.

The excerpt and quotations on page 168 are adapted from "Defense Through Disarmament: Nonviolence and Personal Assault," in *The Universe Bends Towards Justice: A Reader on Christian Nonviolence in* the U.S., edited by Angie O'Gorman (Philadelphia: New Society Publishers, 1990), pages 242–243. Copyright © 1990 by New Society Publishers.

The excerpt on page 173 is from *The Challenge of Peace: God's Promise and Our Response*, numbers 73–74, by the USCCB (Washington, DC: USCCB, 1983). Copyright © 1983 by the USCCB, Washington, D.C. All rights reserved. Used with permission of the USCCB. No part of this work may be reproduced or transmitted in any form or by any means, electronic or mechanical, including photocopying, recording, or by any information storage and retrieval system, without permission in writing from the copyright holder.

The statistics in the "Sexism" sidebar on page 179 are from "Women's Economic Status in the States: Wide Disparities by Race, Ethnicity, and Region," by Amy Caiazza, April Shaw, and Misha Werschkul, Institute for Women's Policy Research Web site, at *www.iwpr.org/publications/pubs/womens-economic-status-in-the-states-wide-disparities-by-race-ethnicity-and-region*.

The statistic on page 179 is from the Havocscope Black Market online database at *www.havocscope.com/blackmarket/prostitution/prostitution-ranking*.

The statistics on page 180 are from "Statistics on Pornography, Sexual Addiction and Online Perpetrators," at *www.safefamilies.org/sfStats.php*.

The statistics in the "Live It!: Avoiding Pornography" sidebar on page 180 are from "Internet Pornography Statistics: 2003," at *www.healthmind.com/s-porn-stats.html*, and "The Effects of Pornography on Individuals, Marriage, Family and Community," by Patrick F. Fagen, at *www.frc.org/pornography-effects*.

The excerpts on pages 182 and 185 are from "Brothers and Sisters to Us: U.S. Catholic Bishops Pastoral Letter on Racism, 1979," at *www.nccbuscc.org/saac/bishopspastoral.shtml*. Copyright © by the USCCB, Washington, D.C. All rights reserved. Used with permission of the

The excerpt on page 185 is from "Pastoral Statement of U.S. Catholic Bishops on Persons with Disabilities," number 6, at *www.usccb.org/prolife/ personswithdisabilities.shtml.* Copyright © 1979 by the USCCB, Washington, D.C. All rights reserved. Used with permission of the USCCB. No part of this work may be reproduced or transmitted in any form or by any means, electronic or mechanical, including photocopying, recording, or by any information storage and retrieval system, without permission in writing from the copyright holder.

The quotation on page 188 is from "Strangers No Longer: Together on the Journey of Hope: A Pastoral Letter Concerning Migration from the Catholic Bishops of Mexico and the United States," number 26, at *www. usccb.org/mrs/stranger.shtml.* Copyright © 2003 by the USCCB, Washington, D.C, and Conferenci a del Episcopado Mexicano. All rights reserved.

The statistics on page 194 are from "World Hunger and Poverty Facts and Statistics 2010," at *www.worldhunger.org/articles/Learn/world%20 hunger%20facts%202002.htm.*

The United States poverty and hunger statistics on page 194 are from the Bread for the World Web site, at *www.bread.org/hunger/us/facts.html.*

The poverty percentages presented in the chart on page 195 are from "The Millennium Development Goals Report, 2010," by the United Nations, at *www.un.org/millenniumgoals/reports.shtml.*

The two mission statements on page 197 are from the Catholic Campaign for Human Development Web site, at *www.nccbuscc.org/cchd/ mission.shtml;* and the Catholic Relief Services Web site, at *crs.org/about/ mission-statement.cfm.*

The statistics on page 199 are from "Income Gap Widens: Census Finds Record Gap Between Rich and Poor," by Hope Yen, at *www. huffingtonpost.com/ 2010/09/28/income-gap-widens-census-_n_741386. html;* and "World's Richest 1% Own 40% of All Wealth, UN Report Discovers," by James Randerson, at *www.guardian.co.uk/money/2006/dec/06/ business.internationalnews.*

The excerpt on page 212 is from "Message of His Holiness Pope Benedict XVI for the Celebration of the World Day of Peace, January 1, 2010," number 7, at *www.vatican.va/holy_father/benedict_xvi/messages/peace/ documents/hf_ben-xvi_mes_20091208_xliii-world-day-peace_en.html.* Copyright © 2009 by LEV. Used with permission of LEV.

The vanishing species statistics on page 217 are from "Extinction Crisis Continues Apace," at the International Union for the Conservation of Nature Web site, at *www.iucn.org/knowledge/news/?4143/ Extinction-crisis-continues-apace.*

The rain forest statistics on pages 217–218 are from the Nature Conservancy Web site, at *www.nature.org/rainforests/explore/facts.html*.

The excerpt on page 218 is from "Message of His Holiness Pope John Paul II for the Celebration of the World Day of Peace, January 1, 1990," number 8, at *www.vatican.va/holy_father/john_paul_ii/messages/peace/documents/hf_jp-ii_mes_19891208_xxiii-world-day-for-peace_en.html*. Copyright © 1989 LEV. Used with permission of LEV.

The quotations on pages 221 and 222 and the excerpt on page 227 are taken from *Renewing the Earth: An Invitation to Reflection and Action on Environment in Light of Catholic Social Teaching*, by the USCCB (Washington, DC, 1992), pages 6, 7, and 14, respectively. Copyright © 1992 by the USCCB, Washington, D.C. Used with permission of the USCCB. All rights reserved. No part of this work may be reproduced or transmitted in any form or by any means, electronic or mechanical, including photocopying, recording, or by any information storage and retrieval system, without permission in writing from the copyright holder.

The statistic on page 224 is from "The Value of the World's Ecosystem Services and Natural Capital," by Robert Costanza et al., in *Nature*, volume 387, May 15, 1997, page 253.

The quotation on page 233 is from "The Aims and Means of the Catholic Worker," in *The Catholic Worker,* May 2008, found at *www.catholicworker.org/aimsandmeanstext.cfm?Number=5*.

The excerpt on page 233 is from "We Appeal to You," by Dorothy Day, in *Catholic Worker*, October 1951, found at *www.catholicworker.org/dorothyday/reprint.cfm?TextID=625*.

The quotation on page 235 is from the Project Rachel Web site, at *www.hopeafterabortion.com/words/index.cfm?page=healing*. Copyright © 2000 Project Rachel.

The excerpt from Thomas Merton's essay "Blessed Are the Meek" on page 237 is reprinted from *Faith and Violence: Christian Teaching and Christian Practice*, by Thomas Merton (Notre Dame, IN: University of Notre Dame Press, 1968), page 18. Copyright © 1968 by the University of Notre Dame Press.

The story on page 239 is based on "Now We Have Leftovers," by Lane Hartill, in *The Wooden Bell*, volume 22 (1), October 2010 (Baltimore: Catholic Relief Services). Copyright © 2010 Catholic Relief Services.

The prayer on page 241 is from the Sr. Helen Prejean, CSJ, Web site, at *www.prejean.org/APrayerFromSHelen.html*. Used with permission of Sr. Helen Prejean, CSJ.

The quotation on pages 246–247 is from the My Hero Project Web site, at *myhero.com/go/hero.asp?hero=womens_peace_movement_liberia_08*.

The excerpt on page 263 is adapted from *St. Benedict's Rule for Monasteries*, translated from the Latin by Leonard J. Doyle (Collegeville, MN: Liturgical Press, 1948), pages 67–68. Copyright © 1948 by the Order of St. Benedict, Inc., Collegeville, MN. Used with permission of Liturgical Press.

To view copyright terms and conditions for Internet materials cited here, log on to the home pages for the referenced Web sites.

During this book's preparation, all citations, facts, figures, names, addresses, telephone numbers, Internet URLs, and other pieces of information cited within were verified for accuracy. The authors and Saint Mary's Press staff have made every attempt to reference current and valid sources, but we cannot guarantee the content of any source, and we are not responsible for any changes that may have occurred since our verification. If you find an error in, or have a question or concern about, any of the information or sources listed within, please contact Saint Mary's Press.

Endnotes Cited in Quotations from Documents Copyrighted by the USCCB

Section 2
1. Cf. *Catechism of the Catholic Church,* 1910.
2. Cf. John Paul II, Encyclical Letter *Centesimus Annus,* 48: *AAS* 83 (1991), 852–854.

Section 3
1. Cf. John Paul II, *Message for the 1999 World Day of Peace,* 11: *AAS* 91 (1999), 385–386.
2. John Paul II, *Message for the 2000 World Day of Peace,* 20: *AAS* 92 (2000), 369.
3. Cf. John Paul II, *Message for the 1997 World Day of Peace,* 3 and 4: *AAS* 89 (1997), 193.
4. Matthew 7:12.

Section 4
1. Cf. John Paul II, Encyclical Letter *Centesimus Annus,* 48: *AAS* 83 (1991), 852–854.

Endnotes Cited in Quotations from the *Catechism of the Catholic Church,* Second Edition

Section 4
1. Cf. *Genesis* 1:26–28.

Section 5
1. *Exodus* 31:17; cf. 23:12.
2. Cf. *Nehemiah* 13:15–22; 2 *Chronicles* 36:21.